Human Nature and Destiny

Edited by

Jean Holm

with John Bowker

PINTER
PUBLISHERS
LONDON, NEW YORK

Distributed exclusively in the United States and Canada by St. Martin's Press

Pinter Publishers Ltd.
25 Floral Street, London WC2E 9DS, United Kingdom

First published in 1994

Distributed exclusively in the USA and Canada by St. Martin's Press, Inc., Room 400, 175 Fifth Avenue, New York, NY 10010, USA

British Library Cataloguing in Publication Data

A CIP catalogue record for this book is available from the British Library

ISBN 1 85567 094 1 (hb)
ISBN 1 85567 095 X (pb)

Library of Congress Cataloging in Publication Data

Human nature and destiny / edited by Jean Holm, with John Bowker,
p. cm. – (Themes in religious studies series)
Includes bibliographical references and index.
ISBN 1-85567-094-1 (hb). – ISBN 1-85567-095-X (pb)
1. Man (Theology) 2. Fate and fatalism – Religious aspects.
3. Personality – Religious aspects. I. Holm, Jean, 1922– .
II. Bowker, John Westerdale. III. Series.
BL256.H87 1994
291.2'2–dc20 94-13747
CIP

Typeset by Mayhew Typesetting, Rhayader, Powys
Printed and bound in Great Britain by Biddles Ltd., Guildford and King's Lynn

Contents

Series Preface

The person who knows only one religion does not know any religion. This rather startling claim was made in 1873, by Friedrich Max Müller, in his book, *Introduction to the Science of Religion*. He was applying to religion a saying of the poet Goethe: 'He who knows one language, knows none.'

In many ways this series illustrates Max Müller's claim. The diversity among the religious traditions represented in each of the volumes shows how mistaken are those people who assume that the pattern of belief and practice in their own religion is reflected equally in other religions. It is, of course, possible to do a cross-cultural study of the ways in which religions tackle particular issues, such as those which form the titles of the ten books in this series, but it soon becomes obvious that something which is central in one religion may be much less important in another. To take just three examples: the contrast between Islam's and Sikhism's attitudes to pilgrimage, in *Sacred Place*; the whole spectrum of positions on the authority of scriptures illustrated in *Sacred Writings*; and the problem which the titles, *Picturing God* and *Worship*, created for the contributor on Buddhism.

The series offers an introduction to the ways in which the themes are approached within eight religious traditions. Some of the themes relate particularly to the faith and practice of individuals and religious communities (*Picturing God, Worship, Rites of Passage, Sacred Writings, Myth and History, Sacred Place*); others have much wider implications, for society in general as well as for the religious communities themselves (*Attitudes to Nature, Making Moral Decisions, Human Nature and Destiny, Women in Religion*). This distinction, however, is not clear-cut. For instance, the 'sacred places' of Ayodhya and Jerusalem have figured in situations of national and international conflict, and some countries have passed laws regulating, or even banning, religious worship.

Stereotypes of the beliefs and practices of religions are so widespread that a real effort, of both study and imagination, is needed in order to discover what a religion looks – and feels – like to its adherents. We have to bracket out, temporarily, our own beliefs and presuppositions, and 'listen in' to a religion's account of what *it* regards as significant. This is not a straightforward task, and readers of the books in this series will encounter a number of the issues that characterise the study of religions, and that have to be taken into account in any serious attempt to get behind a factual description of a religion to an understanding of the real meaning of the words and actions for its adherents.

First, the problem of language. Islam's insistence that the Arabic of the Qur'ān cannot be 'translated' reflects the impossibility of finding in another language an exact equivalent of many of the most important terms in a religion. The very word, Islam, means something much more positive to a Muslim than is suggested in English by 'submission'. Similarly, it can be misleading to use 'incarnation' for *avatāra* in Hinduism, or 'suffering' for *dukkha* in Buddhism, or 'law' for Torah in Judaism, or 'gods' for *kami* in Shinto, or 'heaven' for *T'ien* in Taoism, or 'name' for *Nām* in Sikhism.

Next, the problem of defining – drawing a line round – a religion. Religions do not exist in a vacuum; they are influenced by the social and cultural context in which they are set. This can affect what they strenuously reject as well as what they may absorb into their pattern of belief and practice. And such influence is continuous, from a religion's origins (even though we may have no records from that period), through significant historical developments (which sometimes lead to the rise of new movements or sects), to its contemporary situation, especially when a religion is transplanted into a different region. For example, anyone who has studied Hinduism in India will be quite unprepared for the form of Hinduism they will meet in the island of Bali.

Even speaking of a 'religion' may be problematic. The term, 'Hinduism', for example, was invented by western scholars, and would not be recognised or understood by most 'Hindus'. A different example is provided by the religious situation in Japan, and the consequent debate among scholars as to whether they should speak of Japanese 'religion' or Japanese 'religions'.

Finally, it can be misleading to encounter only one aspect of a religion's teaching. The themes in this series are part of a whole interrelated network of beliefs and practices within each religious tradition, and need to be seen in this wider context. The reading lists at the end of each chapter point readers to general studies of the religions as well as to books which are helpful for further reading on the themes themselves.

Jean Holm
November 1993

List of Contributors

Jean Holm (EDITOR) was formerly Principal Lecturer in Religious Studies at Homerton College, Cambridge, teaching mainly Judaism and Hinduism. Her interests include relationships between religions; the relationship of culture to religion; and the way in which children are nurtured within a different cultural context. Her publications include *Teaching Religion in School* (OUP, 1975), *The Study of Religions* (Sheldon, 1977), *Growing up in Judaism* (Longman, 1990), *Growing up in Christianity*, with Romie Ridley (Longman, 1990) and *A Keyguide to Sources of Information on World Religions* (Mansell, 1991). She has edited three previous series: *Issues in Religious Studies*, with Peter Baelz (Sheldon), *Anselm Books*, with Peter Baelz (Lutterworth) and *Growing up in a Religion* (Longman).

John Bowker (EDITOR) was Professor of Religious Studies in Lancaster University before returning to Cambridge to become Dean and Fellow of Trinity College. He is at present Professor of Divinity at Gresham College in London, and Adjunct Professor at the University of Pennsylvania and at the State University of North Carolina. He is particularly interested in anthropological and sociological approaches to the study of religions. He has done a number of programmes for the BBC, including the *Worlds of Faith* series, and series on Islam and Hinduism for the World Service. He is the author of many books in the field of Religious Studies, including *The Meanings of Death* (Cambridge University Press, 1991), which was awarded the biennial Harper Collins religious book prize in 1993, in the academic section.

Douglas Davies is Professor of Religious Studies in the Department of Theology at the University of Nottingham, where he specialises in teaching the social anthropology of religion. He trained both in theology and social anthropology and his research continues to relate to both disciplines. His interest in theoretical and historical aspects of religious studies is represented in a major study of the sociology of knowledge and religion, published as *Meaning and Salvation in Religious Studies* (Brill, 1984), and in a historical volume, *Frank Byron Jevons 1858–1936, An Evolutionary Realist* (Edwin Mellen Press, 1991). Professor Davies is also very much concerned with practical aspects of religious behaviour and is a leading British scholar of Mormonism and, in addition to various articles, is author of *Mormon Spirituality* (Nottingham and Utah University Press, 1987). He was joint Director of the Rural Church Project, involving one of the largest sociological studies of religion in Britain, published as *Church and Religion in Rural Britain* (with C. Watkins and M. Winter, T. & T. Clark, 1991). As Director of the Cremation Research Project he is conducting basic work on Cremation in Britain and Europe and has already produced some results in *Cremation Today and Tomorrow* (Grove Books, 1990).

Peter Harvey is Reader in Buddhist Studies at the University of Sunderland. His research is in the fields of early Buddhist thought, and the ethical, devotional and meditational dimensions of Buddhism. He has published articles on consciousness and *nirvāṇa*, the between-lives state, the nature of the *tathāgata*, the *stūpa, paritta* chanting, the signless meditations, self-development and not-Self, and respect for persons. Dr Harvey is author of *An Introduction to Buddhism: Teachings, History and Practices* (Cambridge University Press, 1990) and is currently working on *The Selfless Mind: Selflessness and Consciousness in Early Buddhism* (for Curzon Press), and a work on *Themes in Buddhist Ethics* (for Cambridge University Press). He is a Theravāda Buddhist and a teacher of Samatha meditation. He was a member of the CNAA Working Party on Theology and Religious Studies.

Anantanand Rambachan is Associate Professor of Religion and Asian Studies at St Olaf College in Northfield, Minnesota, USA. Dr Rambachan has been working on the interplay between scripture and personal experience as sources of valid knowledge and is the author of *Accomplishing the Accomplished: The Vedas as a Valid*

Source of Knowledge in Sankara (University of Hawaii Press, 1991), *The Hindu Vision* (Motilal Banarsidass, 1992) and *The Limits of Scripture: A Critical Study of Vivekananda's Reinterpretation of the Authority of the Vedas* (University of Hawaii Press). His writing has also appeared in various scholarly journals, including *Philosophy East and West, Religion, Religious Studies*, and *Journal of Dharma.*

Martin Forward is Secretary of the Methodist Church's Committee for Relations with People of Other Faiths, and a Consultant to the Council of Churches for Britain and Ireland's Commission for Inter-Faith relations. He used to work in the Henry Martyn Institute for Islamic Studies, Hyderabad, India. Martin Forward has taught an introductory course on Islam at Leicester University, and now teaches courses on Islam at Bristol University.

Sybil Sheridan is a rabbi and a Lecturer at the Leo Baeck College and the Muslim College, London. She also arranges workshops and seminars on Judaism at Leo Baeck College for Christian theology students and recent ordinands. She is author of *Stories from the Jewish World* (Macdonald, 1987) and contributed two chapters to *Creating the Old Testament* (ed. Stephen Bigger, Basil Blackwell, 1989). Rabbi Sheridan is currently editing a series of texts on women's issues in rabbinic literature and is conducting research on the Song of Songs.

Beryl Dhanjal is a Lecturer at Ealing Tertiary College. She works on the programme for teaching ESOL (English to Speakers of Other Languages) and has special responsibility for developing community links, working mainly with people from the new commonwealth and with refugees. She studied Panjābi at the School of Oriental and African Studies, University of London. She has lectured at St Mary's College, Strawberry Hill, and the West London Institute of Higher Education, and has worked in adult education. She has written and translated many books, and particularly enjoys writing books for children and young people – she has written bi-lingual English/Panjābi books for children.

Xinzhong Yao is Lecturer in Chinese Religion and Ethics, University of Wales, Lampeter. His research interests include classical and modern philosophy, practical ethics, and philosophy of religion and of language; he is currently focusing on comparative philosophy and comparative religion. Dr Yao is author of *On Moral Activity* (People's University Press, Beijing, 1990), *Ethics and Social Problems* (City Economic Press, Beijing, 1989), co-author of *Comparative Studies on Human Nature* (Tienjin People's Press, Tienjin, 1988), *Ethics* (People's Press, Beijing, 1989), co-editor of *Applying Ethics* (Jilin People's Press, Changchun, 1994), and translator of Charles Stevenson's *Ethics and Language* (Social Sciences of China Press, Beijing, 1991). He is a member of the Association of Ethical Studies of China, and Deputy Director of the Institute of Ethics, People's University of China, Beijing.

Wendy Dossett is currently completing Ph.D research in the areas of Japanese Buddhism and religious studies methodology; her main research interests lie in Japanese religion and culture, and the phenomenology of religion. She has worked in Tokyo for the International Buddhist Study Center, an institution dedicated to the translation of Buddhist scriptures. She has lectured on Buddhism in the Department of Religious Studies at University of Wales, Lampeter, and is a tutor in Religious Studies on the International Students' Programme there. Her publications include contributions on Hinduism to the *Chambers Dictionary of Beliefs and Religions* (ed. Frank Whaling, Edinburgh, 1992), and on Japanese religions to *Contemporary Religions: A World Guide* (ed. Ian Harris et al., Longman, London, 1992).

Introduction: Raising the Issues

Douglas Davies

It is in the nature of human nature to possess a destiny. Men and women are not content with a simple awareness of the present. Not only do they reflect upon and interpret their past experiences to produce history, but they also turn to the future and anticipate the unwritten history of what is to be. Destiny is this anticipated future, one that is necessary precisely because human beings also tend to think of themselves as, in some sense, eternal.

From the perspective of the observer, it is the human capacity for creative thought that underlies the idea of both human nature and human destiny. Both are significant, and destiny should not be emphasised at the expense of human nature, even though it is easy to overlook the fact that ideas of human nature are themselves the product of humanity's self-reflection. Every culture has developed its own theory of what makes people human as distinct from animals, or how men differ from women and children from adults. Religions have played an extremely important part in this rise of theories of human nature, but since the eighteenth century in particular, science, psychology and the social sciences have added their own explanations. No account of human nature and destiny can ignore these currents of thought even if they run counter to some religious explanations of life.

There is one distinctive feature above all others which comes from practically all these varied sources, sacred and secular, and which cannot be ignored when discussing human nature and destiny. It is the perception of the dividedness or unsatisfactoriness of life, the human awareness that our destiny is at a distance from present existence, a belief which tends to be explained by defining human nature as intrinsically good or bad.

Inner and outer realities

In terms of religious studies, human nature and destiny can also be approached by realising that inner aspects of human consciousness are the major concern of some religions while others stress the outer domain of the world and of action within it.

One depicts humanity as asleep and needing awakening, another as fallen and in need of raising up. Most of the religions within the Indian and Far Eastern group tend to stress consciousness and mind along with some sort of enlightenment of these dimensions as the goal of existence. Most western religious traditions place their emphasis on the physical world, and the physical body as sites of future restoration and salvation. The distinction between Zen enlightenment and Christian salvation through Christ illustrates these differences. One involves a mental and the other a bodily focus, just as the one does not involve any conception of heaven as a 'place' while the other traditionally has done so. Even so the image of a 're-birth' is as powerfully appropriate in Buddhism as in Christianity, even though the processes behind this term vary. The case of Islam is interesting in that it strongly emphasises resurrection and a life in paradise but interprets people as neither asleep nor fallen but as forgetful and in need of reminding of truth, something which the Prophet Muhammad, the Qur'ān, and subsequent tradition all do.

Secular divisions of humanity

This image of the unsatisfactoriness of life has been mirrored in recent centuries by secular views of human nature and destiny. These provide something of a background against which religions in the modern world have to work out their own ideologies.

Marxist thought, for example, speaks of the alienation of people, and argues for a revolution to create a society where a fulfilment might occur. Moving from the political to the biological realm, Darwin's theory of evolution saw human nature as possessing an underlying animal foundation; later writers have stressed the hunting, territorial and sexual dimensions of this animality – often leading to a distinction between the animal and the human in people. Sometimes this is described as the difference between nature and culture within human beings. This was reflected in sociology when Émile Durkheim described human beings as being *homo duplex* – as possessing two dimensions – the one reflecting society within the individual and the other the more biological life of the individual. For him, human nature came into its own during religious ritual when people felt bonded together and lifted above their ordinary sense of consciousness (1912). In a strongly similar way the psychologist Sigmund Freud analysed people in terms of levels of their mental life, from the rather biological *id* through the *ego* to the *super-ego* which represented the voice of society and its values.

Soul–life–body

One of the most durable descriptions of human nature and destiny comes from a variety of religious views which all share the belief that the physical body is not the entire basis of life but is also, somehow, animated or related to a soul.

The philosophical tradition from Plato in the fifth century BCE, used the distinction between the body and the soul as a basic definition of human nature, one that was radically influential on much of Christianity. Many of the religions reflected in this book possess their own distinctive ways of describing human nature, most of which mirror this sense that there is more to people than meets the eye of ordinary perception. The chapters on both Hindu and Sikh religions put the strong case for the existence of the *ātman*, or Self, as the life-force animating the body. The detailed descriptions of how the soul relates to the body provided by these chapters are all variations on the theme that the soul or life-force is both basic in defining human nature and also fundamental as far as human destiny is concerned. The soul that makes people live now is the source of their ultimate destiny, once it has been subjected to a variety of processes, in relation to reincarnation in the eastern traditions or to some sort of judgement and purgation in the western traditions.

Heaven and hell

The chapter on Islam offers one of the clearest examples of the emphasis upon the body and its resurrection into a new realm of being, depicted as a physical place and distinguished from hell as a site of pain and punishment. Christian history, especially the medieval period, reflects a similar post-mortem geography, with graphic accounts of hell. More psychologically and philosophically influenced versions of these doctrines speak of a necessary purging and transformation of individuals before they can gain heaven itself. The Roman Catholic doctrine of purgatory is a clear example of a doctrine of a sinful human nature whose destiny involves a salvation incorporating a progressive shift to goodness before gaining a full vision of God.

Division and salvation or 'enlightenment'

This dividedness of human nature is often associated with evil or negativity in some way, so that human nature, as we normally experience it, is flawed and imperfect. The Indian traditions talk of it in terms of ignorance and also of illusion or *māyā*, something the Sikhs pinpoint as human self-centredness or *haumai*, while the Judaeo-Christian traditions speak of disobedience and sin. Whatever the precise description, our destiny lies in overcoming this problem by some means or other, and that transcending path is the way of enlightenment or salvation. Sometimes the power to do this comes from within people, as in Zen Buddhism, but many traditions speak of the need for God's transcendent power to bring this about, as in Shinran's Pure Land form of Buddhism. The idea of divine grace summarises this belief and is described clearly but with different emphases in, for example, Christianity, Sikhism and Pure Land Buddhism.

The chapter on Judaism very clearly shows how human life is a 'bundle of contradictions', and how the Jewish tradition has dealt with this through a largely optimistic outlook – from its myths of a good creation through to contemporary life.

Chinese religious traditions present a different picture with, for example, Mencius's stress on human nature's intrinsic goodness, along with theories and ethics fostering perfection in balanced lives set within a unified universe. The question of where unity would be found differs across religions, with the two basic poles of a fulfilment here on earth as in Zen Buddhism or in a heavenly realm of optimum spiritual resources as in Pure Land Buddhism. Similar differences of opinion can be found in Christianity of an otherworldly form, where heaven is the destiny of redeemed people, contrasted with Liberation Theology which emphasises social justice on earth as the focus of the Kingdom of God – a clear example of destiny and morality combined.

Destiny and morality

This relationship between human destiny and morality runs through all the following chapters in some way. The Indian tradition underlying Hinduism, Buddhism and Sikhism is grounded in the idea of rebirth, or re-becoming. The process of *karma* evaluates the life lived and designates the conditions of the next phase of existence in accordance with the moral virtue acquired. In Hinduism, for example, this was traditionally related to the way people fulfilled their moral duties and the obligations of caste membership, and the four stages of life development or *varṇāśrāma-dharma*. In Buddhism it was especially related to observing the precepts – in particular the 'middle way' followed by monks. In Japanese Buddhism this motif interacted with other national characteristics to stress networks of relationships between people as the key theory of human nature, rather than some elaborate analysis of the individual person. Sikhs, by contrast, view the ideal life as that of the married householder living a kind of 'disciplined worldliness'. In a dramatically disarming way, the chapter on Sikhism also surrounds the issue of human nature and destiny with the acknowledgement that 'we do not know why we are here' and adds that it would only be an example of pride for us to think that we did know.

The entry on Judaism takes a different approach, arguing that humanity exists to work within God's creation.

Christianity has varied in the style of life preferred for controlling the body. For centuries celibacy and monastic life were highly praised, while in the twentieth century many Protestant churches place tremendous emphasis upon ordinary family life as the arena for faithful living. It is almost as though the emphasis upon this-worldly ordinariness and the human body has increased as strength of belief in life after death has declined.

The body, sex and gender

Though in the past the soul tended to receive the greater emphasis in accounts of human nature and destiny, the body also remains important. Both the Sikh and Christian accounts speak of the body as an important basis for life, the former seeing some sports as a means of training and disciplining the body, and the latter talking of it as a temple for the Holy Spirit. Several Buddhist and Hindu traditions use the body as the means of developing the inner self, as is obvious in schools of *yoga*.

Two further important dimensions to human nature concern gender and community. Most religious traditions argue that human nature is experienced through being either male or female, with particular responsibilities attaching to each sex. The degree to which each requires the other as part of life-fulfilment varies a great deal and is related to the other dimension – that of community.

In some religions human nature is set firmly within the community base of society, as is dramatically clear in Islam's ideal of the community and Judaism's fundamental belief in Israel as a people in covenant with God. The Japanese creation myths and codes of life reflect a similar corporate spirit, with the nation itself the focus of obligation. Here the lone and isolated individual is quite insignificant in comparison to their position in other religious traditions which stress the importance of individual decision-making by each person before God, as was classically the case in much Protestant Christianity.

Judgement and *karma*

Whether traditions believe in reincarnation under the influence of *karma*, as in the case of Indian and Buddhist faiths, or resurrection in the traditional case of Judaism, Christianity and Islam, they often adopt a doctrine of a judgement after death. This is an idea which can be traced back to the ancient Zoroastrian religion of Persia and to Egyptian religion. Human nature involves a life that is judged, and its destiny hangs on the outcome of that judgement.

One radically important qualification to add to this comes from a belief in divine assistance, benefit, or grace which enables devotees to overcome the punishment which otherwise they would certainly merit. The argument about whether people possess a free will or are predetermined in their actions is also closely linked with this realm of grace as discussed, for example, in Judaism, Christianity and Islam.

Forgetting destiny

Zygmunt Bauman, in an important sociological study (1992), has argued that men and women are human by virtue of their self-consciousness. This not only makes them aware of themselves but makes them aware that they are aware. He believes that this kind of reflexive knowledge lies alongside the profound fact that death brings an end to the thinking self. This truth is too much for people to bear, so they strive to forget about death and organise their social life to cover up the dreadful fact of non-existence. For Bauman, religions are central institutions in this cultural ploy to obliterate what is really known to be true about human nature: that it has no destiny at all. In some respects Bauman's argument resembles Freud's case in *The Future of an Illusion* (London, Hogarth Press, 1973) where he sees religion as a neurosis preventing people from grasping fully the atheist facts of life.

In the future, as often in the past, religious theories of human nature and destiny are likely to be worked out either in a dialogue with, or in opposition to, various secular theories of human nature. This is already becoming increasingly obvious as ethical issues arise from advances in medical science and genetics. So, for example, the chapter on Judaism speaks of God choosing the gender of the sperm in conception, but what will this mean if parents can make the choice themselves – an increasingly likely possibility considering advances in genetics and medicine?

It is possible that just as human cultures have in the past come to explicit knowledge of human nature through religious debates, so too, in the future, they will grapple with the meaning and depth of life through a dialogue with ever-changing religious traditions.

FURTHER READING

Bauman, Z. (1992) *Morality, Immortality*, Oxford, Polity Press.
Durkheim, E. (1912 1st edn) (1976) *The Elementary Forms of the Religious Life*, London, Allen Lane.

1. Buddhism

Peter Harvey

In a survey-book on world religions, Huston Smith[1] starts his chapter on Buddhism with the heading, 'The man who woke up'. This aptly describes the nature of a *buddha*, meaning an 'Awakened One' or 'Enlightened One'. This term implies that most of us – including most Buddhists – are still spiritually asleep. But it also has the implication that all humans are capable of a similar kind of spiritual awakening from the 'slumber' which is our selective, biased and misconceived 'normal' state of consciousness.

The person who became known as 'the Buddha' was Siddhattha Gotama[2] (c. 484–404 BCE). He lived in a period of much religious and philosophical debate concerning the nature of life and its problems. These were highlighted by a breakdown of the values of previously small-scale tribal republics, and the disease and suffering experienced in the expanding cities of the day.

The dominant religious influence then was exerted by the Brahmans, priests of an early form of Hinduism known as Brahmanism. Many Brahmans were still wedded to the mainly sacrificial form of their previous tradition, while others were influenced by the ideas expressed in the *Upsaniṣads*. These related to *karma*, rebirth, and the contemplative quest to attain liberation from the round of rebirths by coming to know *ātman*: one's inner essence, or true Self. There were also those who rejected Brahmanism and sought new ways to find a basis of true and lasting happiness. Such wandering ascetics, or *samaṇa*s, belonged to various groups. The Jains espoused total non-violence and, through ascetic self-discipline and philosophical understanding, sought the liberation of the individual life-principle (*jīva*) from the round of rebirths. The Ājīvakas were fatalists who believed in the cycle of rebirths, but felt that one's form of rebirth was determined by an impersonal 'destiny' (*niyati*). This was in contrast to the belief of Brahmans, Jains and Buddhists that one's rebirth was determined by the nature and quality of one's *karmas*, or actions. Of the remaining *samaṇa* groups, the Skeptics felt that humans could have no knowledge on such matters as *karma* and rebirth, and the Materialists had the view that one was totally annihilated at death. The times were thus ones in which the 'classical' Indian ideas of *karma* and rebirth had not yet been fully established, but were open to debate.

Gotama's entry into the religious scene of his day came after the renunciation of his previous life, as the son of an elected aristocratic ruler. By the standards of his day, he had experienced a life of comfortable luxury. Yet this did not satisfy him: what for many people might be the goal of life was for him the starting point of his spiritual quest. In his twenties, after a sheltered upbringing, he came to realise that even he, in his comfortable existence, was not immune from ageing, sickness and death, so the 'vanities' of youth, health and life left him, and he therefore resolved to take up the life of a *samaṇa*, and join the quest for a timeless imperturbable state beyond change and suffering: *nirvāṇa*.

The problem of suffering later became the focus of Gotama's teaching, once he had found what he saw as its solution. Unlike most other religions, this solution did not involve God – only finite living beings and the overcoming of their weaknesses and limitations, by developing their potential and uprooting their negativities. From the perspective of his teaching, suffering became a stimulus for religious commitment and activity.

As a wandering *samaṇa*, Gotama spent six years trying some of the methods of religious training available in his day. He attained advanced meditative states through *yoga*, but felt that they did not go far enough; he then practised extreme asceticism, but found that such bodily mortification did not bring peace of mind and insight. He therefore set out to develop his own spiritual path. Sitting in meditation, he first established concentration on certain sensations associated with breathing. Then gradually his mind calmed – deeper and deeper, with greater concentration and inner stillness. At a certain point, his mind entered an altered state of consciousness known as the first *jhāna* – a lucid trance in which he was unaware of his surroundings, but intensely aware of his object of concentration. There was thus an uplifting inner quietude and clarity of mind. This process of calming concentration was next taken further to the second, third, and then fourth *jhāna*: a state of profound clarity and stillness, from which even the previous intense joy and happiness had faded away. In such a state, the mind is seen to be a powerful and highly sensitive instrument of knowledge, freed of all the obscurations coming from its normal wandering agitations.

From this state, Gotama then went on to investigate certain aspects of reality, and develop the 'threefold knowledge'. The first was the confirmation, according to his own experience, of rebirth. Pushing his memory further and further back, he is said to have gradually remembered thousands of his past lives. The second 'knowledge' was his confirmation of the principle of *karma*. This was based on his psychic observation of beings dying and being reborn, in line with their past actions. The third 'knowledge' was the most crucial, and concerned his insight into the Four Holy Truths: the heart of his later teaching, focusing on suffering and on its transcending. In attaining this knowledge, he also experienced the goal of his quest, *nirvāṇa*, the ending of all suffering, rebirths and limitations. He was now an 'Awakened One' (Conze et al. 1954: 60–2).

As the Buddhist tradition developed, different schools arose. Of the eighteen or so from the early period, only one survives: the Theravāda or 'Ancient Teaching'. This now exists as the major religion of Sri Lanka, Myanmar (formerly Burma), Thailand, Laos and Cambodia. Around the beginning of the Christian era, a new movement in Buddhism began to develop and then crystalise. This was the Mahāyāna, or 'Great (Spiritual) Vehicle'. Today, this exists as the major religion of Tibet, and one of the main religions of China, Taiwan, Korea, Japan and Vietnam.

The human predicament: the *karma*-rebirth perspective

Much of ordinary Buddhism is in some way related to the ideas of rebirth (*punabbhava*, literally 'rebecoming') and *karma*, for these provide the key framework within which life is understood. The present life is seen as the continuation of a countless series of lives, with no known beginning. The 'explanation' for any one of these rebirths lies in the cravings and energies left over in a being from previous lives, a process which will continue until all their craving-momentum is overcome, by the attainment of *nirvāṇa*. The cycle of rebirth is known as *saṃsāra*, literally 'wandering on' – a process which ambles on and on, indefinitely, with no inbuilt direction or purpose. According to Buddhism, this is the nature of the cosmos. Ultimately, it is an unsatisfactory situation, both in itself, and because of the many forms of suffering that rebirths entail, so that a key Buddhist goal is to transcend it. A lesser, and more easily attainable goal, though, is to act in such a way that one is reborn in the more pleasant realms of rebirth. For most Buddhists, this is their prime goal, along with helping others to do likewise, *nirvāṇa* being a more distant goal in a future life. Among Theravadins, a determined few do aim to attain *nirvāṇa* in *this* life. Moreover, the Mahāyāna has a threefold hierarchy of goals: a good rebirth, personal liberation (*nirvāṇa*), and, highest of all, working for the *nirvāṇa* of all beings, not just oneself, by becoming a *buddha*. The third of these is emphasised by the Mahāyāna, but is also a goal for some Theravadins.

KARMA

If, then, I am a Buddhist, what is seen as deciding the form of my next rebirth? A natural answer would be: 'why, my own actions, my *karma*s'. Broadly speaking, good actions are seen as leading to pleasant rebirths, and bad actions to unpleasant ones. This is not, however, seen as a case of 'rewards' and 'punishments'. A common analogy for *karma* is a seed, and the word for a result of *karma* is a 'fruit (*phala*) of *karma*'. Just as a seed naturally develops into a (plant and) fruit, so an action is seen as naturally leading to a certain kind of result. This all unfolds according to subtle laws of nature, not through the actions of gods or a God. What sets up this chain reaction is the volition behind an action, which is what *karma* is actually defined as being. That volition, with its good or bad motivation, leaves a psychic trace which will sooner or later bring about its results, both in terms of the form of rebirth, and in things which may happen to a person during the present, and future, lives. In this sense, a person is seen as the determiner of his or her own destiny – a destiny defined by the actions which he or she chooses to perform.

Intentional actions are seen as either wholesome/skilful (*kusala*) or unwholesome/unskilful (*akusala*), depending on the nature of the volition. If an action is intended to harm any being, or is motivated by greed, hatred or delusion, it is seen as unwholesome. If it is intended to benefit beings, or is motivated by generosity, kindness or wisdom, it is wholesome (Brown and O'Brian 1989: 58, 85–6). The underlying basis of any unwholesome action is some form of delusion, or misperception of the nature of reality. Actions which are so based are seen as naturally leading to unpleasant results because, so to speak, they go against the grain of reality. Actions related to wisdom and seeing things 'as they really are' have the opposite effect.

Wholesome *karma*s are also said to generate *puñña*, a kind of 'auspicious purifying power' generally translated, not really adequately, as 'merit'. A better shorthand translation is 'goodness-power'. The idea of *karma* helps to motivate both the avoiding of harming others, and also the performance of actions which generate goodness-power, especially those involving generosity to Buddhist monks and nuns. The benefits of goodness-power can be shared with others. In the Theravāda school, the rationale for this is twofold. First, one can invite someone else to rejoice at one's own wholesome action, so that, by their rejoicing-at-goodness, they themselves generate goodness-power. Secondly, if a gift is offered on behalf of someone else, such as a dead relative, it is as if that person is himself or herself doing the auspicious deed. In this way, people can be drawn together in wholesome deeds and in sharing their good effect, and can benefit dead relatives. Mahayanists speak, less guardedly, simply of a 'transfer' of goodness-power to others.

While belief in *karma* can sometimes be used as a cloak for fatalism, it is clear that it is a different kind of concept, and in practice, *karma* is not generally used in a fatalistic way. In Thailand and Myanmar (Burma), for example, good and bad fortune is seen as arising from a combination of past *karma* and present knowledge and effort. Admittedly, people are interested in indications, for example, as given by astrologers, of potential problems on the horizon, but their response to such warnings is not passive. Only when an unfortunate event has actually happened might they put it down to bad *karma* – and thus come to terms with, and then let go of, an unfortunate life event. Until it happens, they do what they can to avert it, using a variety of means including:

1. normal secular effort involving, e.g., medicine or farming techniques;
2. magical means, if these are believed in; and
3. Buddhist means, such as doing good deeds, and chanting protective chants which draw on the beneficent power of the Buddha's words.

According to J. Ingersoll, this produces in rural Thai people an attitude which is 'Hopeful rather than optimistic, positive rather than dynamic, patient rather than assertive', such that they cope with life 'with quiet good humor'.[3] This is in line with a motto on the cover of the Thai-based *World Fellowship of Buddhists' Review*: 'We hope for the best, prepare for the worst, and do whatever is possible'. Nevertheless, some who make their living by unwholesome means, for example, fishermen, will say that it is their *karma* to be reborn into such a community. This is no real excuse, from a Buddhist point of view. Some circumstances one finds oneself in may be due to past *karma*, but one should use one's present freedom to choose so as to try to develop a way of life based on a wholesome livelihood. That said, if an unwholesome action is done due to poverty, it has a less bad effect than if done for mere greed or out of anger.

The *karma* doctrine, of course, has implications for how people with disabilities are thought of. A Buddhist would not tend to see disabilities, particularly those present from birth, as merely accidental – or as a 'gift' from God. They would be seen as the result of previous unwholesome action. This does not mean, though, that blaming disabled people for their plight, or guilt on their part, is appropriate. It is more that their plight is seen as an unfortunate natural result of having acted unwholesomely in the past. There is, however, no reason to look down on the disabled now – the past is the past, and the important thing is how we all act now: both the disabled person him/herself, and those who have dealings with him or her. We all have the same human potential, so should act with generosity and compassion in trying to develop this in ourselves and others. As regards guilt, this is not encouraged by Buddhism. It is good to regret a past bad action, but not to feel heavily 'guilty' about it, for this is a clouded, agitated state of mind not conducive to wholesome action. The important thing is to resolve to act better in the future.

GENDER

According to the *karma*-rebirth perspective, we have all been male and female, many times before. Admittedly, gender has a tendency to stay the same from one life to the next, but it may change if a person has a strong aspiration that this be so, or if the working out of *karma* makes this appropriate. For example, in one text (Norman 1971: 41–4), an enlightened nun recalls some of her past lives, saying that, as a result of once being a male adulterer, some of her future lives were as females in unhappy marriages. In rebirth terms, a female form is seen as slightly less fortunate than a male one, but only because it tends to involve more forms of suffering. These include menstruation, pregnancy and childbirth, and the subordinate position of women in many societies (Woodward 1927: 162–3).

Both females and males are seen as having the same potential for attaining *nirvāṇa*, and it is this which persuaded the Buddha, after initial reluctance, to found an order of nuns (*bhikkhunī*s) as well as monks (*bhikkhu*s) (Conze et al. 1954: 23–6). His reluctance may have been due to its going against the existing view of the position of women in society, or concern about ribald accusations about the relationship of monks and nuns. In any case, he agreed on condition that nuns should follow certain extra rules. Along with the fact that marriage is not a religious obligation in Buddhism, the existence of the order of nuns has helped encourage, in Buddhist societies, a respect for the status of the unmarried woman as an independent agent in her own right. Within marriage, the leader of a household is usually a man, but it can be a woman, and Buddhist women, married and single, are often active in trade and commerce. In cultures influenced by the Confucian social ethic (China, Korea, Japan), though, the actual position of women in society has been clearly subordinate. As to the order of nuns, it survives in China, Korea, Vietnam and Japan but not, in its full original form, elsewhere. In Tibet, the full monastic form for women was never introduced, while in the Theravāda lands of Sri Lanka, Myanmar (Burma) and Thailand, it had died out by the thirteenth century. In all these countries, however, there are female renunciants, generally referred to as 'nuns', following a lesser number of monastic precepts than the full *bhikkhunī*s. At some time in the future, it is possible that the Tibetan and Theravāda *bhikkhunī* form could be revived via the Chinese ordination-line (a valid form requires ordination by *bhikkhunīs* whose tradition goes back unbrokenly to the Buddha).

Psychologically, men and women are seen as tending to have different characteristics, including characteristic strengths and weaknesses. In Tibetan Buddhist symbolism, for example, certain male holy beings represent compassionate 'skilful means' (appropriately adapted ways of helping and teaching people), while their female partners represent intuitive wisdom. Both qualities, though, need to be developed. Nevertheless, it is said that a female can be neither a *buddha* nor a *māra* (a tempter god similar to Satan) (Horner 1959: 109). As gender is changeable from life to life, though, this is no long-term restriction on a person. Moreover, the Theravāda texts refer to many female *arahant*s, or people who have experienced *nirvāṇa*, and the Mahāyāna includes female holy beings among those who are almost *buddha*s (i.e., *bodhisattva*s).

HUMAN, ANIMAL AND OTHER REBIRTH REALMS

Rebirth can be as a human, but also as an animal: land animal, fish, bird or insect. Indeed, it would be said that we have all been animals in some of our past lives, and may well be born again in such forms, depending on the nature of our actions. This implies, of course, that humans and animals are not ultimately different in kind, but differ only in degree. The 'specialness' of humans is expressed, by Tibetan Buddhists, by talking of a 'precious human rebirth', for a human life is a rare and precious opportunity for moral and spiritual development. This should be respected in others and made good use of in one's own case. It is at the human level that most good and bad *karma* is made, for *karma* is intentional, chosen action, and humans have most freedom to choose. To some extent, the higher animals can make some moral/spiritual progress, by choosing, within the limitations of their nature, to act in a less greedy, more giving, less aggressive, and more loving way. In the main, though, animals are creatures of instinct and, according to Buddhism, live out the consequences of the previous bad *karma* which led to their state. In time, the backlog of past good *karma* will raise their state and lead back to a human rebirth.

Human beings may be superior to animals due to their spiritual potential, but they should show their superiority in good treatment of fellow sentient beings, not by exploiting them. The basis of Buddhist ethics is not to inflict on another what one would not like done to oneself (Woodward 1930: 308–11). All beings, human or otherwise, are just like oneself in disliking pain and liking happiness, so, 'Since the self of others is dear to each one, let him who loves himself not harm another' (Brown and O'Brian 1989: 86). Moreover, it is said that, whatever being one comes across will have been, in one or other of one's countless past lives, a close friend or relative (Rhys Davids 1922: 128). As they were good to one then, so one should be good to them now. Thus the most important ethical precept, to 'abstain from injury to living beings', applies to the treatment of both humans and animals. The effect of this, in practice, varies. Certainly a reluctance to kill any being is usual, though this reduces when one gets down to fishes and insects. Avoidance of all flesh foods has not been expected, except in China, Korea and pre-modern Japan. The crucial thing is no direct or instigated killing. Compassion for animals can lead to an old Tibetan lady removing slugs from the middle of the road and giving them some of her apple, or the buying and freeing of captured birds at certain festival times – but only after they have been caught for this purpose!

Less pleasant than an animal rebirth is that of frustrated ghostly beings (*peta*s), and hell beings (Brown and O'Brian 1989: 60–1, 132–3). The latter are seen as living in a state akin to a prolonged, pain-wracked nightmare, as a result of the suffering that they have inflicted on others. In time, though, their hellish rebirth passes; no form of rebirth is seen as eternal, and the only state which is eternal, or rather timeless, is *nirvāṇa*.

Along with human rebirth, the twenty-six forms of heavenly rebirths are seen as comprising the 'good' rebirths. The gods (*deva*s) of these heavens are said to live for nine million human years in the 'lowest' heaven, up to 'eighty-four thousand eons' in the most subtle and refined one. Yet time is said to pass more quickly for them than for humans, and sooner or later they die and are reborn in some other realm. Thus such heavens are *this* side of salvation: they are not ultimate solutions to the problems of existence. Rebirth in them is simply the result of good actions and, as such, they are pleasant, calm and refined forms of existence, but they are still subject to limitations. Nevertheless, gods are less clearly confronted with the limitations of life than humans, human life being less pleasant. So humans are less likely to become complacent, and are thus more likely to be motivated to seek *nirvāṇa*, the 'deathless'.

GODS AND HOLY BEINGS

Despite the limitations of the gods, a traditional Buddhist may seek to interact with them in various ways (Gombrich 1971: 191–213). Only certain versions of western-influenced Buddhism are completely non-theistic, or free of belief in, and recourse to, gods. Traditional Buddhism can be seen as 'trans-polytheistic':[4] accepting many gods, but looking beyond them for what is truly important.

Some of the divine realms are seen as so refined as to be beyond contact with humanity – except by deep meditation. Others, particularly the six lowest, are pleasant realms which are closer in nature to human existence. Buddhists may pray to the gods of these realms in order to bring about worldly benefit, such as good health or a good harvest. In some ways they are looked on in a similar way as politicians: powerful people that one can go to for assistance. They are all seen, though, as inferior in knowledge and influence to the Buddha, and many of the chants which seek their aid ask, in effect, that they give assistance in the name of the Buddha. Some of the gods are specifically said to be followers of the Buddha. Among these are Sakka (or Indra), chief of the pre-Buddhist vedic gods, whom the Buddha converted, and one-time fierce Tibetan gods that were tamed by the eighth century Padmasambhava, so as to become protectors of Buddhism. As Buddhism spread into different cultures, its cosmology had the space to encompass various indigenous gods, from nature deities upwards, provided these were not seen as supreme, eternal beings.

In Theravāda Buddhism, one of the ways of interacting with the gods is to share goodness-power with them, as they will die when their own supply wears out. In return for a share of the goodness-power made by humans, they will offer aid. In Sri Lanka, some Buddhists also take part in the Hindu-based cult of the god Kataragama, going into trances and making vows to the god. Some Theravadins also seek, by good deeds and aspirations, to be reborn in the heaven of the future Buddha, Metteyya (Skt. Maitreya), or to be reborn on earth when he becomes the next Buddha. Metteyya is the only future Buddha referred to in early Buddhist texts but, later,

Theravadins came to add others. For example, in Sri Lanka Viṣṇu, one of the major Hindu gods, is seen as one.

A being working for future Buddhahood is what is known as a *bodhisattva*, or 'Being-for-Enlightenment', and in Mahāyāna lands many of these are believed in (Harvey 1990: 130–3, 182–7; Williams 1989: 228–42). While the Mahāyāna encourages all to tread the path of the *bodhisattva*, those well advanced on this path are seen as existing at a heavenly level, as compassionate beings dedicated to the aid of those in need of help and inspiration. They are thus the focus of prayer and contemplation, and are requested to transfer some of their huge store of goodness-power to their devotees, for their worldly and spiritual uplift.

The Mahāyāna actually sees the historical Buddha as a manifestation on earth of a heavenly Buddha, Śākyamuni, who had already been enlightened for countless ages (Harvey 1990: 125–8; Williams 1989: 167–84). Such a manifestation was to teach and inspire people in the Buddhist way. In the Theravāda view, Gotama did not become a *buddha* until his enlightenment experience at the age of thirty-five. Prior to that, he had been working to develop the perfections of a *buddha* for many lives. At birth he was a (rather special) human, but from the time of his enlightenment he was no longer a 'human' but a *buddha*: an awakened being who, by perfecting his human nature, had transcended it (Conze et al. 1954: 104–5).

The human predicament: the unsatisfactoriness of life

The central 'discovery' of the Buddha's enlightenment experience, and the focus of his first sermon was the Four Holy (or (spiritually) Noble) Truths. These deal with the most important aspects of the nature of the human condition – indeed the condition of all sentient beings – and how to transform this. They comprise the structural framework for all the more advanced teachings of the Buddha, intended for those who have prepared themselves by previous moral and spiritual development. Their form parallels the practice of doctors of the Buddha's day:

1. diagnose a disease
2. identify its cause

3. determine whether it is curable, and
4. outline a course of treatment to cure it.

The first Truth concerns the 'illness' of *dukkha*, the 'suffering' that we are all subject to. The second concerns the key cause of this: craving. The third affirms that by removing the cause of the 'illness', a cure is possible: from the cessation of craving, in the experience of *nirvāṇa*, suffering ceases. The fourth outlines the way to full health: the Holy Eightfold Path, or Middle Way.

In his first sermon, the Buddha formulated the first 'Truth' as follows:

> i) Birth is *dukkha*, ageing is *dukkha*, sickness is *dukkha*, death is *dukkha*; ii) sorrow, lamentation, pain, grief and despair are *dukkha*; iii) association with what one dislikes is *dukkha*, separation from what one likes is *dukkha*, not to get what one wants is *dukkha*; iv) in short, the five groups of grasping (which make up a person) are *dukkha* [numbers added].

Here the word *dukkha* refers to all those things which are unpleasant, imperfect, and which we would like to be otherwise. It is both 'suffering' and the general 'unsatisfactoriness' of life. The first Truth essentially points out that suffering is inherent in the very fabric of life.

The first features described as *dukkha* are basic biological aspects of being alive, each of which can be painful and traumatic. The *dukkha* of these is compounded by the rebirth perspective of Buddhism, for this involves repeated rebirth, re-ageing, re-sickness and re-death. The second set of features refer to physical or mental pain that arises from the vicissitudes of life. The third set of features points to the fact that we can never wholly succeed in keeping away things, people and situations that we dislike, in holding on to those we do like, or in getting what we want. The changing, unstable nature of life is such that we are led to experience dissatisfaction, loss and disappointment – in a word, frustration.

Is Buddhism 'pessimistic' in emphasising the unpleasant aspects of life? A Buddhist's reply is that the transcending of suffering requires a fully realistic assessment of its pervasive presence in life. One must accept one is 'ill' if a cure is to be possible; ignoring the problem only makes it worse. The path to the end of suffering, moreover, is one in which the deep calm and joy of devotion and meditation play an important part. Buddhism, then, does not deny the existence of happiness in the world – it provides ways of increasing it – but it does emphasise that all forms of happiness (bar that of *nirvāṇa*) do not last. Sooner or later, they slip through one's fingers and leave an aftertaste of loss and longing – thus even happiness is to be seen as *dukkha*. This can be more clearly understood when one considers another classification of states of *dukkha*: *dukkha* as physical pain, *dukkha* due to change, and the *dukkha* of conditioned phenomena. When a happy feeling passes, it often leads to *dukkha* due to change, and, even while it is occurring, it is *dukkha* in the sense of being a limited, conditioned, imperfect state – one which is not truly satisfactory. This most subtle sense of *dukkha* is sometimes experienced in feelings of vague unease at the fragility and transitoriness of life.

The human make-up and human potential

A PERSON AS A CLUSTER OF IMPERMANENT, UNSATISFACTORY, NOT-SELF PROCESSES

When the first sermon summarises its outline of *dukkha* by saying 'in short, the five groups of grasping are *dukkha*', it is referring to *dukkha* in the subtlest sense. The five 'groups of grasping' (*upādāna-khandhas*) are the five factors which go to make up a 'person'. Buddhism holds that none of these is free from unsatisfactoriness. Each factor is a 'group' (*khandha*) of related states, and is an object of 'grasping' (*upādāna*) so as to be identified as 'me', 'I', 'myself'. The first is *rūpa*, 'material shape' or 'form': the material aspect of existence, whether in the outer world or in the body of a living being. The second factor is *vedanā*, or 'feeling', whether pleasant, unpleasant, or neutral. The third factor is *saññā*, 'cognition', recognition and interpretation – including misinterpretation – of sensory or mental objects. It is *saññā* which classifies and labels them, for example as 'yellow', 'a man', or 'fear'. The fourth personality factor is the *saṅkāras*, or 'constructing activities'. These comprise a number of states which initiate action, or direct, mould and give shape to character. They include very active states such as determination, joy and hatred, and also more passive states such as sensory stimulation. While some are ethically neutral, many are ethically 'wholesome' or 'unwholesome'. The most characteristic 'constructing activity' is *cetanā*, 'will' or 'volition'. The fifth and final factor is *viññāṇa* '(discriminative) consciousness'. This includes both the basic awareness of an object, and the discrimination of its basic aspects or parts, which are actually recognised by *saññā*. It is also known as *citta*, the central focus of personality, which can be seen as 'mind', 'heart' or 'thought'. This is essentially a 'mind set' or 'mentality', some aspects of which alter from moment to moment, while others recur and are equivalent to a person's character. Its form at any moment is set up by the other mental *khandha*s, but in turn it goes on to determine their pattern of arising – in a process of constant interaction. In the Theravāda, the deepest aspect of 'consciousness' is seen as *bhavaṅga citta*: the latent ground-state of consciousness, which occurs uninterruptedly in dreamless sleep, but is rapidly flicked in and out of in normal consciousness (Collins 1982: 238–47). A similar, but more developed idea is also found in the Mahāyāna philosophy known as Yogācāra or Cittamātra, where there is reference to a kind of underlying unconscious mind, known as the 'storehouse consciousness' (*ālaya-vijñāna*). This stores the effect-potentials of past *karma*s, and then, through the ripening of these, moulds how a person perceives the 'world' (Harvey 1990: 107–9; Williams 1989: 90–3).

Much Buddhist practice is concerned with the purification, development and harmonious integration of the factors of personality, through the cultivation of devotion, virtue and meditation. In time, however, the fivefold analysis is used to enable a meditator gradually to transcend the naive perception – with respect to 'himself/herself' or 'another' – of a unitary 'person' or 'self'. In place of this, there is set up the contemplation of a person as a cluster of changing, conditioned physical and mental processes, or *dhamma*s, thus undermining grasping and attachment, which are key causes of suffering.

The fundamental 'three marks' of all conditioned phenomena are said to be that they are impermanent (*anicca*), *dukkha*, and not-Self (*anattā*). Buddhism emphasises that change and impermanence are fundamental features of everything bar *nirvāṇa*. Mountains wear down, material goods wear out, and all beings die. The gross form of the body changes relatively slowly, but the matter which composes it is replaced as one eats, excretes, and sheds skin cells. As regards the mind, character patterns may be relatively persistent, but feelings, moods, ideas, etc. can be observed constantly to change. It is because things are impermanent that they are also *dukkha* – limited, and potentially painful and frustrating. Moreover, it is said, with respect to each of the five *khandhas*, that if it were truly Self, it would not 'tend to sickness', and it would be totally controllable at will, which it is not (Brown and O'Brian 1989: 50). So, as each *khandha* is impermanent, *dukkha*, and of a nature to change, it is inappropriate to consider it as 'This is mine, this am I, this is my Self'. That is, it is not a permanent, self-secure, happy, independent Self or I.

In the Buddha's day, the spiritual quest was largely seen as the search for, identifying and liberating, a person's true Self (Sanskrit *ātman*; Pāli *atta*) or 'life principle' (*jīva*). Such an entity was postulated as a person's permanent inner nature – the source of true happiness and the autonomous 'inner controller' of action. The Buddha argued that anything subject to change, anything not autonomous and totally controllable by its own wishes, anything subject to the disharmony of suffering, could not be such a perfect true Self. Moreover, to take anything which was not such a Self as if it were one, is to lay the foundation for much suffering. This arises when what one fondly takes as one's permanent, essential Self changes in undesired ways.

The teaching on phenomena as not-Self is not only intended to undermine the Brahmanical or Jain concepts of self, but also much more commonly held conceptions and deep-rooted feelings of 'I'-ness. To feel that, however much one changes in life from childhood onwards, some essential part remains unchanged as the 'real me', is to have a belief in a permanent Self. To act as if only other people die and to ignore the inevitability of one's own death, is to act as if one had a permanent Self. To relate changing mental phenomena to a substantial self which 'owns' them – '*I* am worried . . . happy . . . angry' – is to have such a Self concept. To identify with one's body, ideas, actions, etc., is to take them as part of an 'I' or Self-entity.

The not-Self teaching can easily be misunderstood and misdescribed, so it is important to understand what it is saying. The Buddha accepted many conventional usages of the word 'self' (also *atta*), as in 'yourself' and 'myself'. These he saw as simply a convenient way of referring to a particular collection of mental and physical states. But he taught that, within such a conventional, empirical self, no permanent, substantial, independent, metaphysical

Self could be found. The not-Self teaching does not deny that there is continuity of character in life, and to some extent from life to life, but persistent character traits are merely due to the repeated occurrence of certain *citta*s, or 'mind-sets'. The *citta* as a whole is sometimes talked of as an (empirical) 'self', but while such character traits may be long-lasting, they can and do change, and are thus impermanent – and so 'not-Self', insubstantial. A 'person' is a collection of rapidly changing and interacting mental and physical processes, with character-patterns reoccurring over some time. Only partial control can be exercised over these processes, so they often change in undesired ways, leading to suffering. Impermanent, they cannot be a permanent Self. Suffering, they cannot be an autonomous true 'I', which would contain nothing that was out of harmony with itself. While *nirvāṇa* is beyond impermanence and *dukkha*, it is still not-Self. Though it is unconditioned, it has nothing in it which could support the feeling of 'I'-ness, for this can only arise with respect to the conditioned *khandha*s and it is not even a truly valid feeling there (Collins 1982: 98–9).

The not-Self teaching is not, in itself, a denial of the existence of a permanent Self; it is primarily a practical teaching aimed at the overcoming of attachment. It urges that all phenomena that we identify with as 'Self', should be carefully observed and examined to see that they cannot be taken as such. In doing this, a person finally comes to see everything as not-Self, thereby destroying all attachment and attaining *nirvāṇa*. In this process, it is not necessary to 'deny' a Self; the idea simply withers away, as it is seen that no actual instance of such a thing can be found anywhere.

A common query put to Buddhists is: how can there be rebirth if no permanent Self is acknowledged? For Buddhism, though, after death a person is seen as neither annihilated nor continuing in the form of some permanent Self. The true situation is seen as a 'middle way' between these extremes, in the form of *paṭicca-samuppāda*, 'conditioned arising' or 'dependent origination'. This teaching holds that everything – except for *nirvāṇa*, the unconditioned – arises according to appropriate conditions, and is part of a changing flow of processes. When a person dies, the energy of his or her craving-for-life, and the impetus of his or her past *karma*, causes the stream of consciousness to flow on and find a new life situation. In the case of a human rebirth, conception of a new being occurs in the womb when the appropriate physical conditions come together, along with an available stream-of-consciousness from a deceased being. A new human being then develops in the womb. When born, the individual will have a character and tendencies akin to, and produced by, that of the earlier person. That character will gradually change, though, due to new life experiences and actions.

As death is the most important transition in life, it is seen as important to help a person have a 'good death'. Buddhists thus try to ensure that loved ones die recollecting good deeds, or mentally participating in ones done on their behalf. Monks may be asked to chant near them so that they die in a calm, uplifted frame of mind. In Mahāyāna belief, there is a time-lapse between death and rebirth, and the Tibetans try to guide a 'person' through this period by reading the *Bardo Thotrol* (popularly known as the 'Tibetan Book of the Dead') to them (Conze 1959: 227–32). In the Theravāda, the orthodox view is that the moment of conception immediately follows the moment of death. Nevertheless, early Theravadin texts contain indications that the early Buddhists accepted a between-lives period, and popular Burmese belief refers to a 'butterfly spirit' leaving the body at death to await rebirth.[5] Belief in a between-lives existence can be seen to approximate to western notions of the spirit leaving the body at death. However, a being in such a state is still seen as not-Self, being composed of a number of interacting processes of mind and subtle matter, which condition the following rebirth but no longer exist once it is attained. That is, such a 'spirit' is not unitary or immortal, but a bundle of processes driven on by craving for a new life.

THE 'BRIGHTLY SHINING MIND' AND THE '*BUDDHA*-NATURE'

Given the conditioned, limited nature of the processes comprising a human being, how is it that it is held possible to attain the unconditioned, *nirvāṇa*? One reason is that there is a potential for *nirvāṇa* in the depths of the mind. One early Theravadin text says: 'Monks, this mind (*citta*) is brightly shining, but it is defiled by defilements which arrive' (Brown and O'Brian 1989: 34–5, 71–2). The passage continues by saying that those who know this meditatively develop their minds: implying that they are aware of its potential, usually obscured by defilements such as sensual desire, ill-will and laziness. These arise through the interaction of the mind with the world of the senses – though a newborn baby already has latent defilements left over from previous lives (Horner 1957: 102–3). Many of these defilements have deep roots in the psyche, but the above passage implies that, at the deepest level of the mind, there is great purity and spiritual brightness. Indeed, the passage also refers to the great benefits of meditatively developing lovingkindness, implying that this is a quality already latent in the mind. Human nature may be stained, then, but not indelibly so. This amounts, in effect, to a doctrine of 'original sinlessness':[6] the inherent purity of human nature. The stains are real enough, but the process of removing them from the human make-up is like smelting the impurities out of gold-ore (Woodward 1930: 77–8), the qualities of the pure gold being there all along, waiting to be made available for use.

The potential for transformation, even in evil people, is symbolised in the story of Aṅgulimāla, or 'Finger-garland', a robber-bandit who had the habit of cutting off the fingers of his victims. One day, the Buddha deliberately went out to meet him, as he had intuited that, with an appropriate nudge from himself, Aṅgulimāla could change his ways for the better. The bandit soon saw and chased him, but though the Buddha seemed to walk at only a slow pace, the running Aṅgulimāla was unable to catch him. On telling the Buddha to stand still, he received the reply that *he* should 'stand still' in the harming of living beings. The Buddha's charisma, psychic power of speedy walking, and his teaching, led to a change of heart in Aṅgulimāla, who became his disciple. After ordination and assiduous meditation, he soon attained enlightenment (Horner 1957: 284–9). From a Buddhist point of view, though Adolf Hitler may still have a long period in a hell as a result of his actions, in some future rebirth he will be a human again, and, if he cultivates his seeds of perfection, may one day become enlightened too.

Theravadins see the 'brightly shining mind' as simply the *bhavaṅga* mind (see p. 22). In deep meditation, its purity comes to infuse more and more of the surface consciousness, bringing a clarity and calm which are an ideal basis for developing meditative insight. In the Mahāyāna, the 'brightly shining mind' came to be known as the *Tathāgata-garbha*, the 'embryo' (*garbha*) of the 'Thus-gone' (Buddha). In China, Korea and Japan, this was seen as the *buddha*-nature (Harvey 1990: 113–18; Williams 1989: 96–115; Conze et al. 1954: 181–4, 216–17; Brown 1991). The Indian texts on the *buddha*-nature see it as both a potential to develop, and also as the full-blown perfection of buddhahood, already lying latent within. That is, it has an intrinsic purity, which spiritual practice simply uncovers, an idea particularly stressed in the Ch'an (Chinese) or Zen (Japanese) tradition. As expressed by the famous thirteenth century Zen master Dōgen, Buddhist practice is not in order to *become* a *buddha* – we already are – it is simply to manifest one's intrinsic *buddha*-nature, in more and more of one's life and being.

An alternative perspective, also found in Far Eastern Mahāyāna, is that of the devotional Pure Land schools. These emphasise that the world is now in such a period of moral and spiritual decline that human beings cannot save themselves by their own power. Instead, they must rely on the saving power of the heavenly Buddha Amitābha. Through deep faith in him, the devotee will, at death, be conducted by him to his Pure Land, where the conditions are ideal for attaining enlightenment (Williams 1989: 251–76; de Bary 1972: 197–207, 314–44; Conze 1959: 232–6). Shinran (1173–1263), the founder of the Japanese Jōdo Shin Shu, or 'True Pure Land School', was probably the most extreme of the Pure Land teachers in his condemnation of human nature. He regarded the *buddha*-nature as so deeply buried under the defilements of passion, depravity and ignorance, that humans could be described simply as helpless sinners. Their only hope is complete faith in the saving grace of Amitābha, and avoidance of any vain and ungrateful thought that they could contribute to their own salvation.

The causes of suffering and evil

THE SECOND HOLY TRUTH, ON THE ORIGIN OF SUFFERING

In the first sermon, the Buddha identified the cause of *dukkha* thus: 'It is this craving (*taṇhā*), giving rise to rebirth, accompanied by delight and attachment, finding delight now here, now there . . .'. '*Taṇhā*' literally means 'thirst', and clearly refers to demanding desires or drives which are ever on the look-out for gratification. These lead to suffering in a number of ways. First, they lead to the suffering of frustration, as their demands for lasting and wholly satisfying fulfilment are perpetually disappointed by a changing and unsatisfactory world. Secondly, they motivate people to perform actions whose karmic results lead on to further rebirths, with their attendant *dukkha*. Thirdly, they lead to quarrels, strife and conflict between individuals and groups.

The first sermon identifies three types of craving: for sensual pleasures, for existence, and for non-existence. The second type refers to the drive for self-protection, for ego-enhancement, and for eternal life after death as 'me'. The third is the drive to get rid of unpleasant situations, things and people. In a strong form, it may lead to the impulse for suicide – the rejection of one's whole present life situation. Such a craving, ironically, helps cause a further rebirth, whose problems will be as bad as, or worse than, the present ones. In order to overcome *dukkha*, the Buddhist path aims not only to limit the expression of craving, but ultimately to use calm and wisdom to uproot it completely from the psyche.

Two other important causes of *dukkha* are 'views' (*diṭṭhi*) and 'conceit' (*māna*). The first refers to speculative viewpoints, theories or opinions, especially when they become dogmatic, narrowing a person's whole outlook on life. Such views are seen as hidden forms of self-assertion which lead to conflict with those of other opinions, be this in the form of verbal wrangling or ideological wars and bloody revolutions. Here, it is worth noting that Hitler, Stalin and the Khmer Rouge all had a theory of human nature to motivate and 'justify' their atrocities. The Buddha focused much critical attention on views concerning 'Self'. He felt that these all, in some way or another, located a substantial Self somewhere in the five *khandha*s, so as to lead to attachment.

Deeper than a Self-view, though, is a vague and non-specific feeling of 'I'-ness with respect to the *khandha*s. This is the 'I am' conceit: a deep-rooted self-assertion or egoism, which is concerned about how 'I' measure up to 'others'. So long as such Self or 'I am' ideas exist, one will suffer when what one identifies as 'me' changes or is threatened, and will act in 'self-ish' ways, causing suffering to others. Craving, conceit and views are themselves expressions of, or rooted in, spiritual ignorance – *avijjā* (Skt. *avidyā*). This is the persistent misperception of reality, which continually ignores or overlooks life's indications of the Four Holy Truths, and so mistakenly grasps at things as permanent, satisfying and Self. Thus classical Buddhism does not trace the root of human faults to wilfulness, a concept at the heart of the Christian concept of sin. Shinran's view, though, is similar to this.

MĀRA: THE EMBODIMENT OF EVIL AND DEATH

In its discussion of evil, Buddhism sometimes sees this as personified in the figure of *Māra*, 'Death', or the 'Evil One'. In the simplest sense, he is seen as one of the various gods, who uses the power derived from previous goodness so as to tempt people and keep them within the round of rebirth and re-death. Indeed, he is said to have tried to distract Gotama from his meditations leading to his enlightenment. As with the Christian Satan, a 'fallen angel', he is seen as having had a good past, but uses his power to a perverted end. The sixth heaven, in which *Māra* dwells on the fringes, is the highest of the sense-desire realms, where most beings, including humans, live. All such beings perceive the world in a way largely coloured by the appearance of things as desirable or undesirable. The *brahmā* gods of the next set of heavens, the realm of pure form, perceive the world in a purer, more direct way. *Māra* thus exists at a transition point in the process of spiritual development.

Buddhism sees all the heavenly realms as parallel to certain meditative states. The meditative level corresponding to the beginnings of the pure form realm is the first *jhāna*, or meditative trance. It is attained once the spiritual hindrances of sense-desire, ill-will, laziness, agitation, and vacillation have been fully suspended. *Māra*, in effect, is seen as a being who could not quite make the transition to *jhāna*. Instead of developing power to transcend the realm of sense-desire, he went for power *over* it. This is always a possibility. *Māra*, in fact, is not the name for just one being, but for a kind of being. Like all gods, a *māra* will eventually die, but his position will be later taken over by another *māra*, another being who has fallen into the same trap, and who seeks to entrap others.

At a more philosophical level, *māra* is a term for all that is *dukkha*, all the limited, conditioned processes that make up the world and living beings. Here, it means 'subject to death'. Accordingly, in the Tibetan 'Wheel of Life', a common didactic painting, the various rebirth realms are depicted within a circle held by a demon representing *māra* – illustrating the fact that all rebirths end in death. Popular Buddhism does not refer to *Māra* much, though there is belief in nature deities who may be morally ambivalent, and in need of propitiation. For meditators, though, *Māra* may be a symbolic embodiment of death, and an actual embodiment of human weaknesses, tempting people to fall away from the path.

THE 'PROBLEM OF EVIL'

Over the centuries, Christians have offered many 'solutions' to the theistic 'problem of evil': how can an all-loving, all-powerful, all-knowing God allow evil and suffering in the world? Buddhism avoids this problem by not postulating such a God, and holds that, if a creator-God existed, he would be responsible for the world's suffering. It refers to 'Great Brahmā' as an all-loving god, but one who is limited in power and knowledge. Being mistaken in his belief that he created the world, he is in need of the Buddha's teachings. Suffering and evil, in the Buddhist view, are due to the spiritual ignorance of human beings, and the bad *karma* that they have performed in previous lives. This can even be used to explain the sufferings of animals.

In Mahāyāna Buddhism, though, a problem akin to the theistic problem of evil makes its appearance. The *Ratnagotra-vibhāga* sees the *tathāgata-garbha* (*buddha*-nature) as the basis for all mental activity, including 'unsystematic attention', which wrongly sees the conditioned world as permanent and substantial. This, in turn, is the basis for moral and spiritual defilements. The *Lankāvatāra Sūtra* explicitly says that the *tathāgata-garbha* 'holds within it the cause for both good and evil'. In the final analysis, though, *tathāgata-garbha* thought seeks to avoid the conclusion that genuine evil can come out of the pure *buddha*-nature. Thus the defilements are seen as insubstantial illusions produced by ignorance. Why this exists, though, is a mystery that only a *buddha* can fathom.

Buddhist goals

A good rebirth, and entry into a Pure Land, are Buddhist goals already discussed. What, though, of the ultimate goals of Buddhism: *nirvāṇa* and buddhahood? The Theravāda sees *nirvāṇa* as a transcendent state initially experienced in life, and then finally passed into at death. On attaining it, a person becomes an *arahant*, one who has had all possibility of attachment, hatred and delusion destroyed by the experience (Conze et al. 1954: 42–5; Katz 1982). He or she thus has a radically transformed nature and is imbued with deep, unshakeable calm, profound insight, and warm loving-kindness, coming to fully embody the qualities of the *Dhamma*.

In postulating such a radical transformation of human nature, Buddhism has a very optimistic view of human possibilities, but it sees this as based on a realistic assessment of human weaknesses, their causes, and how to get rid of them. Attaining arahantship takes much dedicated, persistent effort, usually over many lives. But it is seen as a possibility open to all humans. Perhaps the most recent *arahant* in the Theravāda tradition was the Thai meditation master, Acharn Mun, who died in 1949. The path can be begun at any time, and lesser benefits than arahantship, in the form of happier life-experiences, are to be found almost from its start. Prior to arahantship, the most crucial transition on the path is 'stream-entry' (Harvey 1990: 71–2). This occurs when, from sustained meditation, a person gains a first 'distant glimpse' of *nirvāṇa*. By thus attaining the '*Dhamma*-eye' and 'plunging into *Dhamma*', a person enters the 'stream' which will definitely lead to arahantship within seven lives at most. As for the *arahant*, there is no further possibility of rebirth, for all causes of it have been destroyed. When an *arahant* dies, final *nirvāṇa* is entered, and the state of the *arahant* becomes a profound mystery (Harvey 1990: 65–8). The Buddha did not accept that it could be said that the *arahant* beyond death either 'is', 'is not', 'both is and is not', or 'neither is nor is not'. All such notions mistakenly look for some Self-essence in the *arahant*, and wonder what happens to this after death. Nevertheless, it is clear that an *arahant* is seen neither as annihilated at death, nor reborn (as some kind of individual being). Beyond that, perhaps all that can be said is that there is a transcendent, timeless state beyond all suffering.

Both the Theravāda and Mahāyāna traditions agree that an *arahant* has attained a somewhat lesser goal than a perfect *buddha*. In the Theravāda, the difference is, first, that a *buddha* is seen as having more extensive knowledge than an ordinary *arahant* (a *buddha* is also an *arahant*). A *buddha* is also seen as rediscovering the timeless *Dhamma* or Truth at a time in human history when it has been forgotten. Teaching it, he makes it possible for others to come to know and experience it, and so become *arahants*. For the Theravadin, only a few beings need take the longer path, to perfect buddhahood – and some Theravadins have done this. It is best, though, that most seek to practise the *arahant*-path already made available by Gotama Buddha. In the Mahāyāna tradition, a *buddha* is seen as a glorious and omniscient heavenly being, who can live for countless eons before finally passing into final *nirvāṇa* (Harvey 1990: 125–33; Williams 1989: 167–84). He is also seen as compassionately sending down help to those in need of assistance and teaching: Gotama Buddha is seen as one such manifestation. Nevertheless, Mahayanists emphasise that all have a duty, at some time, to tread the long path to perfect buddhahood, for the universe contains countless worlds, and there will always be a need for more *buddha*s to teach and help beings. Those who dedicate themselves to the path to buddhahood are said to be *bodhisattva*s, 'Beings-for-Enlightenment'. These are seen as more compassionate than *arahant*s, for they are willing to spend longer in the round of rebirths, giving help to suffering beings. In stage six of their ten-stage path, they reach a level akin to that of the *arahant*s, but rather than then transcending rebirth, they continue, in the form of heavenly saviour beings, until finally ripe for buddhahood. Yet prior to this, they still know *nirvāṇa*. In the Mahāyāna perspective, *nirvāṇa* is, in an ultimate sense, not different from the conditioned world of *saṃsāra*. This is because investigation of the make-up of the conditioned world reveals a mysterious 'emptiness', which cannot be differentiated from the 'emptiness' that is *nirvāṇa*, and also 'buddhaness' (*buddhatā*). Here, 'emptiness' is a term indicative of the lack of inherent nature or essence in anything, which means that the true nature of reality cannot be captured in human language and concepts (Harvey 1990: 95–104; Williams 1989: 55–76). The *bodhisattva*, then, is one who increasingly comes to know the nirvanic dimension of the world, and who aids other beings in maturing their *buddha*-nature.

Solutions to the human predicament

In the scheme of the Four Holy Truths, the solution to the problems of life, encapsulated in the word *dukkha*, is the practice of the Holy Eightfold Path. The Path has eight factors, each described as right or perfect (*sammā*):

1. right view or understanding,
2. right directed thought,

3. right speech,
4. right action,
5. right livelihood,
6. right effort,
7. right mindfulness, and
8. right concentration.

These factors are also grouped into three sections (Horner 1954: 362–3): 3–5 pertain to *sīla*, moral virtue; 6–8 pertain to *samādhi*, meditative cultivation of the heart/mind (*citta*); 1–2 pertain to *paññā*, or wisdom. The eight factors exist at two basic levels, the ordinary, and the transcendent or holy, so that there is both an ordinary and a Holy Eightfold Path (Horner 1959: 113–21). Most Buddhists seek to practise the ordinary Path, which is perfected only in those who are approaching the lead-up to stream-entry. At stream-entry, a person fully enters the Holy Eightfold Path.

At the 'ordinary' level, the Path-factors are as follows. 'Right understanding' (*sammā-diṭṭhi*) relates mainly to such matters as *karma* and rebirth, making individuals take full responsibility for their actions. It also covers intellectual, and partial experiential, understanding of the Four Holy Truths. Right-directed thought concerns the emotions, with thought rightly channelled towards peaceful freedom from sensuality, and away from ill-will and cruelty to lovingkindness and compassion. Right speech is the well-established abstaining from lying, back-biting, harsh speech and empty gossip. Right action is abstaining from wrong bodily behaviour: onslaught on living beings, taking what is not given (theft and cheating), and wrong conduct with regard to sense-pleasures (adultery, etc.). Right livelihood is avoiding ways of making a living which cause suffering to others: those based on trickery and greed (Horner 1959: 118), or on trade in weapons, living beings, meat, alcoholic drink, or poison. Right effort is directed at developing the mind in a wholesome way: avoiding and undermining states of mind which express attachment, hatred or delusion, and meditatively developing and stabilising wholesome states of mind. Right mindfulness (*sati*) is a crucial aspect of any Buddhist meditation, and is a state of keen awareness of mental and physical phenomena as they arise within and around one. Right concentration (*samādhi*) refers to various levels of deep calm known as *jhāna*s: states of inner collectedness arising from attention closely focused on a meditation object. At the 'holy' level, moral virtue becomes spontaneous, and right understanding is true wisdom – knowledge which penetrates into the nature of reality in flashes of profound insight, directly knowing the world as a constant flux of conditioned phenomena.

The order of the eight Path-factors is seen as that of a natural progression, though neither the ordinary nor the holy Path is to be understood as a single progression from the first to the eighth factor. Once developed, the Path-factors mutually support each other to allow a gradual deepening of the way in which the Path is trodden. In terms of the division of the Path into virtue, meditation and wisdom (always given in this order), the Path can be seen to develop as follows. Influenced by good examples, the first commitment will be to develop virtue – a generous and self-controlled way of life for the benefit of self and others. To motivate this, there will be some degree of preliminary wisdom, in the form of some acquaintance with the Buddhist outlook and an aspiration to apply it, expressed as *saddhā* – trustful confidence or faith. With virtue as the indispensable basis for further progress, some meditation may be attempted. With appropriate application, this will lead to the mind becoming calmer, stronger and clearer. This will allow experiential understanding of the *Dhamma* to develop, so that deeper wisdom arises. From this, virtue is strengthened, becoming a basis for further progress in meditation and wisdom. With each more refined development of the virtue–meditation–wisdom sequence, the Path spirals up to a higher level, until the crucial transition of stream-entry is reached. The holy Path then spirals up to arahantship.

In the case of the Mahāyāna *bodhisattva*-path, the transition from its 'ordinary' version to its 'holy' version is the 'path of seeing', the first full experience of 'emptiness'. To be ready for the *bodhisattva*-path, a person must be prepared by prior spiritual training, and should then contemplate the plight of suffering beings, and the need for *buddha*s to help them. This prepares the mind for the experience of the arising of the 'thought of enlightenment' (*bodhi-citta*), the heartfelt aspiration to strive for buddhahood for the sake of others (Brown and O'Brian 1989: 152–68). The aspirant then takes various *bodhisattva*-vows to strengthen his or her resolve. In the Chinese tradition, these vows are part of the ordination ceremony for monks and nuns. The *bodhisattva* path consists, essentially, of the compassion-motivated development of six 'perfections' (*pāramitās*): generosity, virtue, patience, vigour, meditation and wisdom (Harvey

1990: 121–4; Williams 1989: 204–14). Most of their content has parallels in the Theravāda tradition, but Mahayanists see the underlying motivation as loftier. At the heavenly level, the *bodhisattva* fulfils four more perfections before final buddhahood is attained.

The above says little about devotion, but most Buddhist schools see this as a very useful preliminary and complement to other aspects of practice, as it develops a warm and pure heart and strengthens aspiration. (See the chapter on Buddhism in *Worship* in this series.) Ultimately, though, it must itself be complemented by wisdom based on direct experience. The Mahāyāna provides a greater range of objects of devotion, in the form of the various heavenly *buddha*s and *bodhisattva*s; but Theravadins can equally develop great joy in their devotion to Gotama Buddha, both because of the teachings he gave to the world, and the goal that he embodied. In the Pure Land schools of Far Eastern Mahāyāna, devotion to Amitābha Buddha overshadows and sometimes replaces all other practices. This is expressed mainly through the medium of the oft-repeated chant *Nama Amida Butsu* (Japanese form), 'Hail to the Amitābha Buddha!'. Through this, a person can let go of 'self-power' – any attempt to improve or save oneself by one's own power – and open up to the saving 'other-power' of Amitābha. The Japanese Nichiren school also emphasises devotion, though as a form of self-power. This is done by chanting *Namu myōhō renge kyō*, which focuses on the truth-power embodied in the text known as the *Lotus Sūtra*.

For an ordinary Asian Buddhist, practice consists of some mixture of: generation of goodness-power by supporting monks and contributing to Buddhist festivals and ceremonies; chanting in order to draw down the blessings of the Buddha's Truth, or of the heavenly *buddha*s and *bodhisattva*s; devotional/contemplative chanting; making offerings before *buddha* images; showing respect to and listening to the teachings and chanting of monks; keeping the ethical precepts; meditation on loving-kindness, or on a compassionate *bodhisattva*; and perhaps calming meditation on the breath. If commitment becomes stronger – or if family tradition urges it – a person may become a novice (prior to the age of twenty), or a monk or nun.

Monasticism was part of Buddhism from the very beginning, though originally the monks and nuns followed a wandering, rather than a settled life (Harvey 1990: 73–5, 217–43). Becoming a monk involves shaving the head – as a sign of the renunciation of vanity – taking a new name, wearing a monastic robe and, most important of all, committing oneself to over two hundred monastic rules of training. These include ethical rules on such matters as non-violence and non-stealing, rules of self-discipline concerning complete sexual abstinence and fasting after noon, and rules aimed at producing calm and graceful behaviour. All are intended to aid the monk in becoming aware of, and gradually dealing with, the cravings, attachments and irritabilities that are part of human nature. This process is also aided by the chanting, study, work and meditation that are part of monastic life. Lay people look to monks and nuns as inspiration, as teachers and advisers, and as focuses of religious giving, so as to generate goodness-power. They also go to them for the performance of a variety of rituals, such as the chanting of blessings, and, in Tibet, the performance of mystery plays. Monks may also act as educators, astrologers and, to some extent, doctors, to the laity. In Japan, however, Buddhism has become more lay-centred, particularly since a government decree in 1872 that all monks (but not nuns) could marry. Most now do so. Thus, the only real Buddhist monastics in Japan are now the nuns, and young men in training for becoming priests – essentially ritual specialists. Post-war Japan has also seen the development of a number of lay-led movements which are seeking to relate Buddhism in new ways to the needs and aspirations of an industrialised urban people.

In Theravāda countries, in Tibet, and to some extent in China, Korea and Vietnam monasticism remains at the heart of Buddhism. It is the focus for the more intense Buddhist training, and the preserver, transmitter and re-invigorator of the tradition. It supports and inspires lay practice, and its members guide and serve the laity in a range of ways. Perhaps the most archetypal relationship between the laity and the *saṅgha*, or monastic community, is that of alms-giving. In this, the lay householder gives material support for a way of life based on renunciation and 'homelessness'. In 'return' the lay-person experiences the joy of giving to wholesome recipients, thus generating much auspicious, purifying goodness-power. This is seen as leading both to material benefits, such as good health and success, and to spiritual uplift. Of course, some monks take to monasticism as a lazy way of life, and some laity have a rather acquisitive attitude to accumulating goodness-power, but such is human nature!

NOTES

A pronunciation guide for Pāli and Sanskrit words is found in Harvey (1990: xxi). As an initial guide, note that a, i and u are pronounced short unless they have a bar over them (ā, ī, ū), in which case they are pronounced long (as are e and o). C is pronounced ch, th as an aspirated t, ph as an aspirated p, ṣ as sh and ñ as ny.

1. (1958) *The Religions of Man*, New York, Harper Colophon, p. 80.
2. Pāli version; in Sanskrit Siddhartha Gautama. In general, Pāli versions of terms are used here, except in a few cases where the Sanskrit versions have become well established in the literature. Thus *karma* (Pāli *kamma*), *nirvāṇa* (Pāli *nibbāna*), *bodhisattva* (Pāli *bodhisatta*). Names of Mahāyāna texts and holy beings are also in Sanskrit. Pāli is the textual and liturgical language of Theravāda Buddhism, while a form of Sanskrit was the original language of most classical Mahāyāna texts, which now exist mainly in Chinese and Tibetan.
3. 'Fatalism in Village Thailand', in *Anthropological Quarterly*, 39: 224.
4. Smart, N., 'Problems of the Application of Western Terminology to Theravāda Buddhism', in *Religion*, Spring 1972: 39.
5. Spiro, M. (1971) *Buddhism and Society*, London, George Allen and Unwin, pp. 85 and 249–53.
6. Cousins, L.S. (1973) 'Buddhist Jhāna', in *Religion*, 3: 117.

FURTHER READING

de Bary, W.T. (1972) *The Buddhist Tradition in India, China and Japan*, New York, Vintage Books [translations from all schools; includes useful introductory essays].

Brown, B.E. (1991) *The Buddha-nature*, Delhi, Motilal Banarsidass.

Brown, K. and O'Brian, J. (eds) (1989) *The Essential Teachings of Buddhism*, London, Rider [translated extracts plus comments, all schools].

Collins, S. (1982) *Selfless Persons: Imagery and Thought in Theravāda Buddhism*, Cambridge, Cambridge University Press.

Conze, E. (1959) *Buddhist Scriptures*, Harmondsworth, Penguin, [translations from all schools].

Conze, E., Horner, I.B., Snellgrove, D. and Waley, A. (1954) *Buddhist Texts Through the Ages*, New York, Harper and Row [translations from all schools].

Gombrich, R. (1971) *Precept and Practice: Traditional Buddhism in the Rural Highlands of Ceylon*, Oxford, Clarendon.

Harvey, P. (1990) *An Introduction to Buddhism: Teachings, History and Practices*, Cambridge, Cambridge University Press.

Horner, I.B. (1954, 1957, 1959) *Middle Length Sayings*, Vols I, II, III, London, Pali Text Society [translations of *Majjhima Nikāya*, from Theravāda Pāli Canon].

Katz, N. (1982) *Buddhist Images of Human Perfection*, Delhi, Motilal Banarsidass.

Norman, K.R. (1971) *Elders' Verses*, Vol. II, London, Pali Text Society [translation of *Therīgāthā*, a collection of verses by enlightened nuns from Theravāda Pāli Canon].

Rhys Davids, C.A.F. (1922) *Kindred Sayings*, Vol. II, London, Pali Text Society [translation from *Saṃyutta Nikāya*, from Theravāda Pāli Canon].

de Silva, P. (1979) *An Introduction to Buddhist Psychology*, London, Macmillan.

Suzuki, D.T. (1983) *An Introduction to Zen Buddhism* (3rd edn), London, Rider.

Williams, P. (1989) *Mahāyāna Buddhism: The Doctrinal Foundations*, London, Routledge and Kegan Paul.

Woodward, F.L. (1927, 1930) *Kindred Sayings*, Vols. IV, V, London, Pali Text Society [translation from *Saṃyutta Nikāya*, from Theravāda Pāli Canon].

2. Christianity

Douglas Davies

For Christians, human nature and destiny are to be understood through the doctrines of creation and salvation. Traditionally speaking, God creates and sustains the world and humanity. Human beings, both through their own God-given freedom and from the actions of others, experience evil. They are saved from the consequences of sin by Jesus Christ who is believed to be both human and divine, and who conquers sin and death through his own death and resurrection. God is committed to humanity and to a future kingdom of moral righteousness, and believers are called to work for this goal through the Church which already symbolises God's work.

This world view is drawn from the Bible which itself clearly poses and sets out to deal with the great issues of human nature and destiny. 'What is man that Thou art mindful of him?', asks the Psalmist in Psalm 8, which is a good place to begin exploring the Christian view of life's meaning, reminding us, as it does, that Christianity owes much to Jewish scriptures as a basis for later Christian thought.

This Psalm begins with the glory of God expressed in the grandeur of the heavens with moon and stars all speaking of God through their very existence. It is in the light of this wonder and magnificence that the question of human significance is raised. What can human life in all its apparent smallness mean when set against the immensity of the heavens? The Psalmist answers that humanity is made by God and placed in dominion over the 'work of God's hands' in the form of the animals of earth, sea and sky. Humanity itself is part and parcel of the wonder of the creation, but a part given special responsibility for the earth.

So it is that the doctrine of creation answers human self-reflection. But, if the Psalmist centuries before Christ could be moved to question human significance in the light of the dome of heaven, how much more demanding this question becomes after the modern scientific revolution in understanding the immensity of space and of the universe. Can men and women, boys and girls, not to mention plants and animals, have any significance when we think of our earth as the smallest of small flecks in an unimaginably immense universe? For most ordinary people untrained in astronomy, physics or mathematics, the size of the universe simply does not make sense – it is too big to understand, we have no way of comparing it with anything. And even when scientists say that it is statistically very probable that there are other civilisations out there in the universe, we find it hard to understand or accept. Because such descriptions of the cosmos give to human nature and destiny a dimension that many individuals find impossible to understand, significance is lost within the vastness of it all. The key issue of the relevance of persons is brought into sharp focus, and, as far as Christian theology and faith are concerned, becomes vitally important.

Persons at the heart of everything

Many things in life depend upon our perspective, not least the significance of the universe where size on the one hand, and personal significance on the other, give two potentially different outlooks.

We have already said that if size is the basis of judgement, then men and women count for infinitesimally little on the scale of the universe. But if we ask about significance, we can say that human beings are the most important part of the universe since it is humans who are doing the thinking about space and time.

This raises a curious fact that is often overlooked, namely that it is these large-brained human animals' own reflections upon the size of the universe that make them feel insignificant. It is as though the very genius of thought turns against itself, but only if size is the key consideration.

If love, or human relationship, or scientific discovery, or poetry, or any other creative product of human life is taken as the basis for judgement, then human beings come to assume immense importance when compared with millions of light years of dust-strewn space.

Christian belief has firmly embraced this issue of perspective, and has appreciated the issue of the immensity of the heavens against the smallness of human stature. The outcome of its reflection on the problem has resulted in a commitment to the doctrine of creation. And that doctrine allows both for the immensity of the universe in terms of size, and the immensity of human beings in terms of self-conscious life. Human nature involves life in an immensity of space, it involves the drive to try to understand the physical universe, and it also involves the rise of worship of the God who could make both the great size of space and the worth of human personality.

This worth of human beings was central to the world view of European Christianity for many centuries, with the Bible-fed belief that the earth, as humankind's home planet, was the centre of the universe. It has often been fashionable to criticise this view and say that humankind had an inflated image of itself and, like a spoiled child, wanted to be at the centre of everything. More realistically, we should appreciate that the biblical myths of creation as spelled out in Genesis inevitably fed the view of human priority, and nothing in human experience contradicted it.

INTERPRETING EXISTENCE

It is more than likely that these creation stories were read by many generations of Christians as factual accounts of human origins. It made very good practical sense to think of human nature as created by God and, following human disobedience and the entry of sin into the world, as redeemed by God through Jesus. The picture painted by Paul in his Epistle to the Romans draws close parallels between the first Adam who sinned and Jesus as the second Adam who redeemed humankind. This world-view accorded with human experience of wickedness and of forgiveness, as well as answering the obvious question of life's significance.

The traditional Christian interpretation of existence possessed an explanation for moral evil within itself. It is perfectly understandable that the Genesis creation stories should have been read in a literal way as explanations of life. Other parts of the Bible, especially the New Testament, played a further part in explaining what happens after this life. The accounts of the resurrection of Jesus and beliefs about life in heaven after death complemented the Christian theory of life, especially when read in an equally literal way. Human nature and destiny could be adequately explained through the Bible.

INTERPRETING THE WORLD

Copernicus and Darwin stand out as two scientists who helped alter this world view, but many theologians of the nineteenth and twentieth centuries went further in changing the way we understand the biblical accounts of creation and life. Copernicus (1473–1543) was a canon of Frauenberg Cathedral in Prussia who had studied astronomy and mathematics in Poland and Italy. He came to realise that the sun was the centre of the solar system, a view that contradicted the age-long theory that the sun went around the earth. This finding laid the foundation for other discoveries about the universe which, in a philosophical sense, can be said to have shifted humankind from the centre of the universe. This astronomical outlook has come to be very influential in the birth of the 'size and distance' perspective on human life.

More dramatically still, Charles Darwin (1809–1882) altered the way people understand themselves. From his work on evolution it became increasingly obvious that humans had an animal ancestry. While the Bible spoke of all living things coming from the dust of the earth and, in that sense, having a common identity, evolution spoke of a more direct form of descent. From the later nineteenth century and throughout the twentieth century the animal nature of humans has assumed an increasingly important place in human self-knowledge and self-discovery.

For some people these two perspectives – Copernicus on cosmic size and Darwin on animal ancestry – have been highly influential in forming an overall perspective on human nature which differs from the biblical picture of humankind as a special creation. Instead of God creating a universe as a home for human beings, there emerges a picture of an unexplained universe in which the human species simply happens to have evolved.

INTERPRETING THE BIBLE

At the same time that Darwin was fostering the idea of evolution, some biblical scholars and theologians were studying the Bible and producing a new more liberal view of it than traditionally had been held by Christians. At the centre of this new form of biblical criticism was the issue of myth and history, with a stress on the various sources or documents from which the Bible was derived, rather than on the idea of divine revelation and authority lying behind the scriptures.

Hermann Hupfeld (1796–1866), for example, wrote in 1853 an important study on the sources underlying the book of Genesis. Still better known are Julius Wellhausen (1844–1918), who was concerned with the way Jewish institutions and ideas had developed through history, and Hermann Gunkel (1862–1932), whose work in the history of religions led him to talk about the ways in which the Israelites adopted and transformed beliefs that originated in other religions. These, along with other forms of biblical study and criticism, deeply influenced the way the Bible is interpreted and understood. This applies as much to the creation stories in Genesis as to any other part of the Bible. For some Christians, this involves a major problem, especially when questions of biblical criticism are placed alongside scientific accounts of creation and both are seen as attacks upon traditional Christian explanations of the origin of human life.

Creation or evolution?

'Creation or evolution?' – this stark opposition is often presented as the choice Christians have to make when they decide on the meaning of life. But the apparent simplicity of this three-word phrase hides a series of complicated issues that need to be spelled out.

The first issue involves the word 'creation'. It is surprising how often people, even moderately well-educated individuals, assume that orthodox Christians believe that God actually created the universe in six days. There is no doubt that some Christians do believe in a six-day creation, especially those who would be happy to call themselves fundamentalists and who believe that the literal meaning of biblical passages is the best way of understanding them. There are many problems involved with this approach to the Bible, however, including the fact that there are two creation accounts in the first two chapters of Genesis which approach the idea of God's creation of humankind in rather different ways.

The first account (Gen. 1: 1–2, 3) gives an orderly and sequential account of what God did on each 'day' of creation, including the fact that the sun and moon were created on the fourth day, leading up to the creation of male and female on the sixth day. In the second creation story, the male human being is created on the very first day when 'the Lord God made the earth and heavens' (Gen. 2: 4). The man is taken and placed in the garden of Eden, and only after all the other plants and animals are made does Eve, the first woman, get to be made from one of Adam's ribs (Gen. 2: 21). The differences between these two accounts of creation are quite stark, and show how inappropriate it is to try to harmonise them into a single scheme. It becomes doubly difficult to try to harmonise them with certain geological theories about different rock strata as some people have occasionally tried to do.

The most obvious way to understand these passages is to see them as myths of origin which deal with different themes and which seek to establish some basic values. Both make it obvious that God is responsible for the universe, and that humankind's existence is not accidental or arbitrary. They also emphasise the divine command that humanity should obey God and act responsibly in the world. But the first account works out these ideas in an orderly progression of events, while the second puts the male–female relationship at the centre of the story.

Many Christians would be happy to see these stories as contributing to their knowledge of God, and of human life lived in obedience to God, without taking them in a literal way. Instead of reading the accounts as some sort of history or science, they take them as theological statements about the human condition. The stories are seen as answering the 'why?' of creation rather than the 'how?' of creation. They remind us that another aspect of the 'creation or evolution' distinction lies in the fact that, since the nineteenth century, certain ideas have actually changed their meaning or have come into existence for the first time. The theory of evolution, for example, has changed the way many people understand human, animal and plant life. Similarly, the very idea of history and the way people tell stories and build up religious and other texts has been transformed. This means that modern interpreters have to choose between many different categories of literature when trying to understand a text that has come down from much earlier times, when these categories were not explicitly understood. This is a difficult point to make clear but it means, for example, that at a time when science did not exist as we know it today, it would be natural to accept a mythological explanation for something because no other explanation existed. Given the modern choice between science and myth, and many other categories of classification, more sophisticated descriptions are possible.

CREATION THROUGH EVOLUTION

For many modern Christians, the choice between creation and evolution is unnecessary, accepting as they do that the Genesis stories deal with religious truths about God and humanity while scientific theories attempt to explain how the universe has come to be the way it is. For them, creation is achieved through evolution.

But this perspective has its own problems, because, if Christians hold to it, they do so believing that God intended to create humanity. An evolutionist who is speaking only in scientific terms can make no such statement of belief and can only assume that what emerges through evolution does so in an accidental way. Some scientists have even spoken in more recent years about what they call the 'anthropic principle', the idea that the universe is not random and works in such a way as to produce humankind. This view would certainly not be acceptable to the majority of scientists, but it shows that even scientific interpretations can vary.

Many modern Christians have accepted the evolutionary and scientific view of the way the universe works, and some have found their own theological thinking stimulated by it. It is worth considering several trends that have come from this sort of scientific perspective, because they deeply influence Christian ideas on human nature and destiny.

The challenge of evolution

It is hard for late twentieth-century people to grasp the impact made by evolutionary thought on their nineteenth-century forebears. So many new ideas have emerged in the twentieth century that we have become familiar with novelty and quickly take for granted something that was quite unknown only decades earlier. This is especially true in science and technology, two areas that radically influence human life in both great and small ways. For example, the discovery of DNA, as the chemical basis of human chromosomes containing the basic biological information on the make-up of individuals, took place in the late 1950s and by the mid 1960s the topic was on the syllabus for sixth form pupils. By the 1970s it formed part of popular knowledge about life processes.

When Darwin published his discoveries on evolution in *The Origin of Species* (1859) and *The Descent of Man* (1871), he was presenting material that dramatically altered the way human life was understood. He was also shifting the goal-posts as far as the origins of human life and identity were concerned. It had been customary to think of the origin of humanity in terms of a direct and immediate special creation of God. The biblical stories of Adam and Eve and their descendants underpinned many ordinary people's world view, as well as the thinking of most church leaders. To have this long-standing assumption challenged was a major problem because it raised the issue of authority. What was the basis of truth about life? What was human nature? What source of information and method of study should be followed to know the truth about humanity?

For many centuries theologians had debated with philosophers about the nature of life, but always it was one person's opinion against another. And more than that, there was the weight of tradition and social influence that came from the churches to back-up ideas drawn from the Bible and from earlier church authorities. Complex webs of influence linked churches, schools and colleges, powerful families, moral rules and the secular law makers.

With Darwin and several other important thinkers of the mid- and late-nineteenth century, science began to emerge in a quite new way as a source of authority about life and the world. This was also the period when industry and engineering were making western nations uniquely powerful and wealthy, and making Britain's the greatest Empire in the world. Science was able to demonstrate its discoveries and not simply to argue them as earlier critical philosophers had done.

The Bible and theology were set against scientific theory and the laboratory. It is no wonder that some church leaders quite simply set themselves against this new knowledge and argued that it was godless. But it is even more important to appreciate that some Christian thinkers saw these discoveries as valuable insights into the way God worked in the world. Rather than turn their backs on evolution, they eagerly explored it and sought to apply it in Christian reflection on the world and on human life. For them the question of human nature and destiny at the beginning of the twentieth century had to be approached in quite different ways than had been appropriate in the eighteenth or any earlier century. Many churches of the late-twentieth century are still coming to terms with this fact, and the challenge is still dramatically insistent.

Some evolutionist Christians

The following individuals are a few among many who have taken up the challenge of evolutionary ideas and used them in developing their own theological perspective on human nature. Each one went in a different direction and with a different purpose, and they are useful examples because of their varied emphasis. Jevons was concerned with social life, morality and the individual. Whitehead with a philosophy of the universe, and Teilhard with the spiritual life and with Christ.

JEVONS 1858–1936

F.B. Jevons was English and spent his whole life as a university teacher in the University of Durham. He began teaching Latin and Greek with a deep interest in philosophy, but rapidly came to see the importance of evolutionary ideas in the development of religion and human personality (1896, 1906). The new discipline of anthropology caught his attention, and he used it to produce some of the earliest studies of the evolution of religion, belief and faith. Evolutionary theory provided Jevons with the key to understanding the emergence, through various stages of primitive and world religions, of the kind of human personality capable of love, service and self-sacrifice. Such a personality was, he believed, also able to understand God in increasingly clear ways. This sense of revelation coming through the natural religion of humankind was very important to Jevons because he did not want to make any distinction between natural religion and revealed religion.

On a more religiously conservative front, another English scholar,

L.S. Thornton, also took the perspectives of modern science in a serious way and related them to the tradition of Christian theology, and especially to the theology of the church and society. Like Jevons, Thornton's work has been largely forgotten, but it offers a good example of a serious Christian thinker seeking to relate theology to science in order to understand more of human nature within the overall activity of God (1950).

Unlike Thornton, who was an Anglo-Catholic priest and scholar, Jevons was a liberal in theological terms, and found that experience in relation to social life and ethics was a vital element in his thinking (Davies 1991). He was more concerned with what a person felt than with some abstract notion of what a person ought to think. In the evolution of religion Jevons believed there was also a development in what people felt of God, an intuitive foundation for their lives and for their theology.

WHITEHEAD 1861–1947

Alfred North Whitehead was a mathematician and philosopher but he became committed to an evolutionary view of the universe and humanity (1926). Because he spoke so much of the process underlying the universe and its development he, and other theologians such as Charles Hartshorne (1967), Schubert Ogden (1979) and Norman Pittinger (1967), were called Process Theologians. One concern of this perspective is to see the universe as full of potential which is in the process of being worked out in an open and dynamic way and in close relationship with God. This dynamic aspect of God's being reflects the belief that these processes of change all take place 'in-God'.

God is not far removed and untouched by events in the universe but is, in some sense, part and parcel of them. For Process Theology, the main focus of Christian 'tradition' lies in the present rather than somewhere deep in the past, and Christians have to be aware of the present activity of God in and through the evolutionary processes of life which go on to influence humanity's destiny. Love and the love of God are key ethical and theological features in Process Theology, and touch upon the way people live and interpret their lives.

TEILHARD DE CHARDIN 1881–1955

Pierre Teilhard de Chardin was a French Jesuit who spent much of his earlier life in China working as a physical anthropologist on human evolution, and his later life in the USA working for an anthropological research foundation. The Roman Catholic Church in France was suspicious of some of his work because he sought to interpret theology through the idea of evolution.

For him, humanity is caught up in both a material and a spiritual realm, though few are aware of it. God is forever stirring up the universe through divine activity within it, and is leading the universe and humankind onwards to a future goal which is love. Christ as the risen Son of God is the 'Omega Point', the centre of this creative power. As far as Teilhard was concerned, he even thought that for a fuller scientific understanding of evolution this theological belief ought to be given some part to play. Christ was the focus of love, and gave meaning to the universe as it developed and progressed into the future and into God. In other words, it is wrong to split science off from religion, with one explaining the 'how?' and the other the 'why?' of the universe and of life. For Teilhard, there is a unity between God's purpose and energy within creation and Christ's power of love within salvation. This sense of unity is part of his deeply mystical and poetic sense of the presence of Christ within the universe and within his own consciousness (Chardin 1965), that is basic to Teilhard as a priest and as a scientist. But this perspective of Teilhard's originates in and through faith, and not through the traditional methods of science, so there is no way in which it could be taught as a standard scientific approach. In fact, it raises the question of faith, which needs to be considered in its own right at this point because, as far as the Christian tradition is concerned, faith lies at the heart of both human nature and destiny.

Belief and faith in human nature

Belief is a complex thing. From a practical point of view it involves an intricate combination of reason and emotion, set within the life context of each individual. The element of reason concerns thought and logical reflection, and can be developed through study and training. Emotion, by contrast, involves a complicated bundle of processes involving the human capacity for insight, along with moods and feelings that surround our experiences in life. Belief involves all of these three factors of reason, emotion and autobiography.

Belief is central to the Christian view of human nature. Men, women and children are persons capable of belief and of a knowledge of God. For Christianity, belief represents a fuller and more intensely human life than a life lived in disbelief. This is because belief involves the rational acceptance that the universe is created by God and is therefore an intelligible place in which to exist. But it also involves the sense of trust in God as redeemer. Disbelief or unbelief is regarded as a negative feature.

Faith and unbelief need to be considered together because human nature and destiny cannot be understood apart from faith and the nature of God; indeed, in many respects the Christian idea of human nature is determined by the Christian doctrine of God.

GOD AS CREATOR

In Christian thought, God is uncreated, and is the source of all things. Human nature is part of a world which is part of a cosmos that is entirely God's responsibility. Whichever particular theory is held about how God created the world, the fundamental Christian belief is that God is the Creator. And as creator, God sustains the creation. In many respects the first creation myth in Genesis can be misleading when the idea that God 'rested on the seventh day' is taken literally. Many contemporary Christians would want to talk of the creator as constantly involved in and with the creation so that it is sustained at every moment by God. This makes the changes and developments which are still occurring part of the creative activity of God.

HUMANITY AND THE IMAGE OF GOD

Because men and women are said to be made in the image of God (Gen. 1: 27), they too have a responsible part to play in the ordering of creation. This idea of being made in the image of God has been taken from Chapter 1 of Genesis and interpreted in different ways within the Christian tradition. In part, it embraces the rule and dominion given to humankind by God (Gen. 1: 28), but it has also been seen to lie in human reason, in the moral sense and in creativity. In more literal interpretations of Christianity, it has even been understood as a physical resemblance, a view which comes to full expression in the Mormon doctrine which says that God actually possesses a body which is the model of the body of human beings.

One major feature of the image of God that has tended to differentiate Catholic from Protestant theology is the question of how much the image was influenced by the Fall. Here there are several strands of argument to contend with, because the major issue lies in the idea of a historical Fall of Adam. In much early traditional theology the idea of a historical Adam and Eve was largely accepted in a natural way; until the nineteenth century, both Catholic and Protestant theologians were agreed on this point. Where they disagreed was on what happened at the Fall. One particular point of contention was whether the image of God, whatever it was, had been completely erased or merely, in some way, flawed and impaired.

In the light of modern science and technology, the interpretation which emphasises the creative aspect of human reason has an important part to play alongside the moral aspect of life. Now, more than ever before in human history, human beings can actually engage in a direct form of altering and manipulating aspects of the world, as in genetic engineering. The moral dimension of human nature, however, does not seem to evolve to produce saints at anything like the same speed that reason evolves in its process of discovery. It is to this moral realm of sin that we now turn.

Sin and evil

While the creation stories of Genesis do talk of God as creator and of the world as a perfect place, they quickly pass on to speak of evil as a radical flaw running through the otherwise perfect creation. This flaw has two aspects to it. On the one hand, temptation seems to come to human beings from beyond themselves, and on the other, it emerges from within individuals.

THE DEVIL

The external source of evil is symbolised in Genesis by the serpent (Gen. 3: 1), which seems to be an independent agent, throwing a question mark over what God has said. In other biblical passages this personalised focus of evil appears as Satan (Job 2: 1 ff.) or the Devil, and by the time of the New Testament writers, this picture of the devil as an enemy of God and source of problems for humanity is widespread. At the outset of his ministry, Jesus is said to have been tempted by the devil in the wilderness (Matt. 4: 1 ff.). Similarly, in their turn, Christians are exhorted to resist their adversary, the devil (Jas. 4: 7), who prowls around as a lion seeking his prey (1 Pet. 5: 8). In the Apocalypse this evil figure reappears as the ancient serpent, the devil, and Satan, the deceiver of the whole world (Rev. 12: 9).

However portrayed, the figure of the devil expresses the belief in a real power of evil that is set against good. J.B. Russell's study *The Devil* (1977), traces the many ways in which believers and professional theologians have described or tried to interpret this awareness of evil.

POSSESSION

At times in the history of Christianity the sense of the objective existence of the devil has been very strong, as in the fifteenth-century Inquisition with its belief that witches actually did enter into pacts with the devil and needed to be punished for this for the good of their eternal souls.

A belief in the devil, along with a belief in evil spirits, has also played a part in the practical faith and spirituality of some modern trends of contemporary Christianity. The Charismatic Movement, for example, which emerged and grew dramatically from the 1960s in the USA, in Britain and in many other developed countries, was, in part, associated with a belief both in the devil and in evil spirits. This belief could take the dramatic form of serious possession by the devil, requiring exorcism.

It is interesting to see this attitude emerge in the later twentieth century which is often considered to be a more secular age. Still, with the growth of popular cinema and video, there has been a spate of films which have brought the idea of an objective, evil force vividly into the everyday world of ordinary people. In the 1970s, for example, the Church of England became increasingly aware of popular beliefs in evil spirits, and encouraged each diocese to appoint a priest with special responsibility for this area. In practical terms this sort of 'ministry of deliverance', as it was often called, embraced a wide variety of behaviour, including experience of ghosts or frightening presences as well as the fear of some who had engaged in seances or games seeking to contact spirits.

Within some Charismatic Churches the idea of possession could take a rather different form, with the belief that particular Christians could come under the influence of various sorts of 'spirits', such as the spirit of rebelliousness or apathy. This shows how wide the idea of spirits and spirit influence can be within Christian Churches, varying from a full sense of devil possession, requiring a major and formal exorcism, to a state that is more of a personal disposition (or even clinical illness) interpreted almost metaphorically as 'possession' or evil influence.

SELF-POSSESSION

In their own way these ideas also raise the issue of human nature and how it functions. They show, too, how Christians can differ in interpreting human life. For just as there are those who believe in the objective existence of evil spirits and the devil, there are many others – and certainly they would be in the majority among professional Christian leaders – who hold no such belief.

The language used about evil is very important for the way believers understand and interpret their lives. Many Christians do not accept the objective 'existence' of the devil or of evil spirits, yet still talk of evil, as in the example provided by Paul Tillich's (1886–1965) twentieth-century existentialist theology. He chooses to speak of the 'demonic–tragic structures of individual and group life', and not of the devil or of evil spirits. Tillich sees this demonic element embracing, 'disruption, conflict, self-destruction, meaninglessness, and despair in all realms of life' (Tillich 1953: 55).

This focus makes individuals more responsible for their lives, and does not shift blame to the devil, or even to God, by saying that God may tempt them to do something. In practical terms this is important because failure to take responsibility for our own temptations and sense of sin makes it more difficult to face up to problems and to take decisions for ourselves. In the New Testament, the Letter of James gives clear voice to this very issue: 'each person is tempted when he is lured and enticed by his own desire' (Jas. 1: 14).

SPIRIT-POSSESSION: ANTHROPOLOGY AND CHRISTIANITY

Any serious discussion of spirits and spirit-possession in Christianity cannot be separated from the kinds of issues studied in social anthropology. Social anthropologists rightly and properly work on the basis of practical disbelief in the gods and powers acknowledged in different human societies. By doing this, anthropology can focus on the social forces at work in people's lives and on the cultural expression of human beliefs.

It is interesting to see some of the patterns and trends that emerge, even though human beings are so diverse that numerous exceptions can often be discovered. So, for example, beliefs in spirits can be taken as expressions of evil and of negative life experiences and pressure, as Ioan Lewis argued for possession cults in some Islamic groups in Africa. So among some Somali wives, spirit possession was a way of allowing them to exert pressure on their husbands to pay attention to them and to their needs (Lewis 1986: 94 ff.).

In an interesting study of women in South Wales, the medical anthropologist, Vieda Skultans (1974), showed how women were the regular clients of male mediums through whose state of trance and contact with the spirit world some benefit was brought to the women. She interpreted this situation as one where women gained some consolation from contact with the sensitive male medium in contrast to the lack of personal concern shown them by their husbands. In this case, there is no full-scale possession by spirits but there is a belief in spirit involvement with the life of human beings.

What is particularly significant is that, in this context, human life is understood against the complex and mysterious backcloth of spirits, mediums and trance states. In other words, human nature cannot be understood in and of itself but only with the help of some additional forces of a spiritual and personal nature.

Many other examples of various kinds of possession could be given to show that it tends to be particular individuals in particular social situations who experience a sense of possession. From the perspective of social anthropology, possession is not a random event. This helps us see how much social life affects human nature, and brings us to the radically important theological point that a major dimension of human nature is social.

Human nature is social

One of the most fundamental Christian beliefs about human nature is that individuals belong together as a community of people. One of the Genesis myths makes this dramatically clear when God says, 'It is not good for man to be alone' (Gen. 2: 18), and goes on to create a partner to establish humanity as male and female. Much of the rest of Genesis is taken up with an account of the kinship groups, clans, and finally a nation which God establishes as part of a covenant relationship. The Jewish religion and culture born from this divine endeavour was community-minded to its core, as the Ten Commandments make crystal clear, spelling out each person's social obligations and duties.

The emergence of Christianity continued this theme, with the covenant relationship between God and Israel opened up to all humankind. The Acts of the Apostles drives home this conviction that people from 'every nation under heaven', whether Jews or gentiles, were open to the salvation provided by Jesus Christ (Acts 2: 5; 10: 1 ff.).

Just as the congregation of faithful Jews meeting in the synagogue expressed the community nature of Hebrew religion, so the emergence of the company of believers meeting as a church expressed the Christian commitment to life as a social fact. Paul helped to forge early Christian ideas to a great extent, and the idea of Christians as the body of Christ firmly reinforces this corporate image of human life as social life. When Paul says, 'You are the body of Christ and individually members of it' (1 Cor. 12: 27), he is not simply talking about being a member of a group; he is taking the idea of a human society further by linking it with Christ. This is one reason why the church is sometimes called a supernatural society or a spiritual society. This is especially true for Christians who interpret the world and Christian life in a sacramental way, seeing material things as symbolic of divine truth. The Christian socialist thinker,

F.D. Maurice (1805–1872), pinpointed the family and the nation as two 'spiritual orders' which indicated the nature of human nature as intended by God. In his influential book, *The Kingdom of Christ* (1837), he argued that the church took up and transformed these basic institutions to ensure that they did not turn in on themselves and become negative and destructive features of life.

SERVICE AND FULFILMENT

Profound ethical consequences flow from this social view of the world and life. Service to God involves a service to our neighbour and to society at large. Human nature comes into its own when it gives itself to others. The idea of self-sacrifice as an ethical principle of Christian living comes to be seen as intrinsic to human success and fulfilment because the individual is turned from self-concern and self-obsession to a concern for others. This has become an integral part of Christian spirituality as a basis for ethics, and often surfaces in prayer and worship, as in the well-known prayer of Saint Francis, where he asks God to grant that 'we may not seek so much to be consoled, as to console; to be understood as to understand; to be loved, as to love; for in giving we receive, in pardoning we are pardoned'.

Service is about the relationships we have with others and, more specifically, about the quality of those relationships. It is tied to the Christian idea that service to God is both a kind of slavery and a kind of freedom. This underlies the history of Christian churches in their charitable work through hospitals, schools and places of refuge for the needy. Though dramatically evident in European society in earlier centuries before modern states took over these welfare duties for their citizens, these ideals of service and care remain a key Christian concern in the modern world, especially in developing countries. This concern for people is not without a reason, and it too plays an important part in the Christian idea of human nature – human worth.

Human worth in human nature

In terms of Christian understanding, all human beings have an intrinsic worth, for the three basic reasons: God creates them; God in Christ loves and redeems them; and, being made in God's image, they are persons in their own right. One of the central tasks of Christianity is to teach people that they have a worth because God sees them in a positive way and calls them into a sense of their own significance.

CREATION AND MYSTERY

The processes of creation give to human beings a sense that the universe is not a random and meaningless background to their own meaningless lives. This is not to say that atheists are all, necessarily, despondent people. It is possible for someone who does not acknowledge a creator to be fascinated and absorbed by life and the nature of the universe. That same fascination has an important place in Christian thought, too, because religious belief does not immediately make everything obvious and clear as far as the universe is concerned.

Though from some simple, and perhaps fundamentalist, perspectives religious belief may clarify all the universe's intricacies, for many other Christians the universe and life itself possess a tremendous mystery and wonder. The essence of human nature involves this sense of mystery about reality.

The fact that a Christian may believe that God is involved with this creation and is active within it can add to the mystery, precisely because there is a personal element, a sense of expectation, surrounding the meaning of life. It is in this sense that belief in the universe as made for us possesses an integrity rather than a selfish self-centredness.

GOD IN CHRIST LOVES AND REDEEMS

The central message of Christianity is that the God revealed in creation as an outgoing source of life, is also revealed in salvation as an outgoing source of love. The universe reveals God's creativity, and Jesus reveals the divine love. The belief that God engages with sin and evil through the life and work of Jesus is taken by Christians to show the personal nature of God. Evil and sin are moral ideas and relate to the experience of persons, so it is that, in and through a person described theologically as the Son of God, God encounters these things – a point that is so important that we return to it below when considering the Incarnation.

One important question in Christian theology concerns 'theodicy', or the problem of evil. In essence, it asks how a good and almighty God can allow dreadful suffering in a world for which he is responsible. Christianity responds to this great problem by talking of God being involved in the suffering of the world through Jesus. In a formal sense the question is side-stepped and not answered, but for many, the example of Jesus' suffering and a sense of God's presence with them in their suffering are a practical way of coping with their own problems of evil.

GOD'S IMAGE AND PERSONAL WORTH

Despite the Fall, however it is interpreted and understood, men and women still have the capacity to be creative and loving people, even though they may sometimes choose to be destructive and hateful. Human life is precious because of this capability. In strictly biological terms, it is true that any particular individual could turn out to be astonishingly gifted, so that every child should be cherished because of that fact. But in terms of Christian morality and ethics, all human life is precious because it expresses the divine creativity.

It is this conviction that lies behind the argument that some Christians expound over abortion, and all Christians share in concern for the deprived, oppressed and poor. As children of God, all are valuable. It is an idea inherent in the teaching of Jesus, when he says that things done to others can be understood as things done to him (Matt. 25: 35). This identification of Jesus with other people brings us to the doctrine of the Incarnation, which is the key issue for a Christian understanding of human nature and destiny.

The Incarnation and human life

Several important councils of early church leaders, especially the Councils of Nicea in 325 and Chalcedon 451, established the doctrine that Jesus of Nazareth was both fully human and fully divine. This was no easy conclusion to arrive at, and the way to it was strewn with many variant attempts at defining and explaining just who and what Jesus was. All this is perfectly understandable given the Jewish background of strong monotheism alongside beliefs in a coming Messiah and in intermediary figures between God and humanity (M. Casey 1991).

The Council of Chalcedon, for example, argued forcefully that Jesus should be viewed as being one person having two natures – both a human nature and a divine nature. This commitment to the belief that Jesus was both human and divine came to typify mainstream Christian orthodoxy even though it has sometimes proved difficult, if not impossible, to spell out in any real detail the 'chemistry or biology' of how this was possible. More than anything else, the deity and humanity of Jesus expresses a belief in his uniqueness and in his competence to be the saviour of the world.

Perhaps one of the most interesting aspects of these debates about Jesus Christ – Christological debates as they are called – is that they do two things at once. They talk about God and they also talk about humanity. The question of human nature is at the very heart of Christological debates, not simply the nature of Jesus, but the nature of all people. To talk about Christology is also to talk about what is called 'theological anthropology', i.e., the doctrine of human life and nature.

This becomes particularly apparent through one of the major theological concerns of the Councils that produced the creeds: the belief that though Jesus was fully human he was sinless. Such a contrast between this one man and all other human beings highlights the place of sin within ordinary human nature, and defines the relationship between Jesus as the saviour and the rest of humanity. Here human nature is defined by contrast with the nature of God which is sinless. And yet, at the same time, it outlines the human vocation to be sinless, and therefore the process of salvation.

SIN IN HUMAN NATURE

We have already seen the centrality of sin to the Christian doctrine of human nature; it is one point on which most Christian traditions are largely in agreement. The very heart of the Christian message lies in seeing Jesus as the saviour of sinners. Sin itself has to do with the way individuals understand and treat both themselves and others, and most especially how they relate to God.

Basic aspects of sin in the Christian tradition involve human disobedience to God, grounded in human self-love. Pride is thought to be so deep-seated that the self is placed before God and before other people. Humility is the opposite of this, and puts both God and others before the self; but humility cannot emerge and develop of its own accord because of the flawed quality of human nature. This flawed nature of things is related to the idea of the image of God, the *Imago Dei*, in which humankind is said to have been created (Gen. 1: 27).

In all of its meanings the *Imago Dei* has been a very important issue in the history of Christian theology, lying as it does at the heart of differing doctrines of salvation. It is also important because the idea of creation underlying it is rather literal in its reading of the Bible and assumes that humankind was initially made perfect and existed in a state of original righteousness. This involved a closeness of relationship to God prior to a fall into sin through disobedience. Theologians have discussed various consequences of this Fall on the image of God in humankind. For some, the image was totally destroyed through the Fall; for others, it remained but only in a distorted and mutilated form. For the early Fathers, for medieval theologians like Thomas Aquinas, and for Reformation theologians, the idea of the Fall as being a historic event is an important implicit assumption. After the period when God and humanity were closely related, there came a time when sin caused a separation and distance between them.

The Incarnation, then, becomes doubly important – not only as the means for God to share in human nature, through Jesus of Nazareth, to save humankind, but also as another momentous event in humanity's history when the Fall is reversed and the image of God is visible once more. Jesus is seen as the 'Second Adam' who achieves where Adam failed:

> For as by one man's disobedience many were made sinners, so by one man's obedience many will be made righteous.
>
> (Rom. 5: 19)

Death is seen as the outcome of the Fall and of the sin of Adam. The spoiled image of God is overtaken by death. But resurrection and eternal life come through the obedience of Jesus as the second Adam, who is the very image of God because he is himself divine. The following quotation shows how part of the New Testament sees the idea of the image of Adam as a negative and sorry thing, but the image of Jesus as its saving correction: 'Just as we have borne the image of the man of dust, we shall also bear the image of the man of heaven' (1 Cor. 15: 49).

In Jesus, the image of God is restored to humanity and, through the work of the Holy Spirit, individual men and women, boys and girls, can come to share in its restoration:

> And we all . . . beholding the glory of the Lord are being changed into his likeness from one degree of glory to another.
>
> (2 Cor. 3: 18)

Processes of salvation

Although they all agree that this depends upon the grace of God, churches differ in how they think grace works. The Catholic traditions stress the sacraments; from baptism through to the last rites, the grace of God is passed to people through the sacraments of the church administered by priests. Protestants emphasise the inner working of the Spirit in relation to the teaching and the preaching of the Bible, and allied to a conversion of the individual, while the Greek Orthodox traditions emphasise the resurrection power of Christ to bring all people to share in God's life and nature.

One of the great historical debates on sin and salvation asks whether human beings can themselves aid the process of salvation. In the fifth century Augustine, Bishop of Hippo, and Pelagius, a British monk, argued this case. Augustine said that humans could do nothing to advance their own cause as far as salvation was concerned; God does it all by grace. Pelagius argued that God had given people the capability to do good if only they would do so. The essence of the argument is found not only in the New Testament (Rom. 5; Jas. 2: 17, 18) but also later, in the Reformation, when Luther echoes Paul and Augustine in seeing God as the sole source and means of salvation.

So it is that human nature and destiny lie within the scheme of sin and salvation. But to many modern thinkers the framework of a historical Fall is unacceptable, especially if the Genesis accounts are regarded as mythical material. This is where another approach to the human predicament is useful and needs careful exploration.

HUMAN EXISTENCE AND SALVATION

Just because Adam and Eve may be regarded as figures in a myth does not mean that the Fall ceases to be theologically important. The human experiences of alienation from others and from God, of being inwardly divided and emotionally torn, of being lost and a stranger in life, all speak of that flaw which is at the heart of fallenness. So too does an awareness of guilt and shame over one's life and actions. The moral sense surrounding us in society, and especially in Christian teaching, and even within our own conscience, brings us to a knowledge that we are divided beings. As Paul expressed it, 'I can will what is right but I cannot do it' (Rom. 7: 18).

This led Paul, and after him both Augustine and Luther, to dwell on and to develop the doctrine of predestination – the idea that we are all so lost and dead in sin that God alone can bring life to us. The pathetic moral weakness of human nature in its fallen state – irrespective of whether we believe in a historic Fall or simply see the Fall as a way of describing the way we are now – depends on divine help. Unless God specifically wills our salvation, we would be ultimately and certainly lost. Luther spoke of people as being 'curved in on themselves'. This deep awareness of one's plight lies at the heart of the sense of gratitude to God for taking us in hand and drawing us out of ourselves and into Christ.

The doctrine of predestination is usually associated with the idea of free will, and with the strong belief that we are so helpless that even our will is corrupt and cannot bring about the good we might believe we ought to do.

Although many look upon predestination as a negative and unfortunate doctrine that causes some Christians to be rather over-sure of their own salvation and overly eager to see others as damned, it is more properly to be seen as a means of gratitude to God for saving helpless people. This can be seen theologically in the doctrine of double-predestination developed by John Calvin

(1509–1564), whereby God was believed to predestine some people to salvation and others to damnation. Karl Barth's twentieth-century theological position changed this quite dramatically, as he focused predestination within the person of Jesus. Jesus is the one predestined to death and also to life.

HUMAN DESTINY AND JESUS CHRIST

Jesus is the measure of humanity and the ground of its destiny. This centrality of Jesus as both God and Man is quite crucial for understanding the Christian view of human nature and destiny.

In some ways this is a strange emphasis, since humans are defining themselves in terms of what they are not. The one who is taken to be the model human being is everything that ordinary human beings are not. Formal theology strongly argues that Jesus was like us in every respect except that he did not sin. In practical terms this is difficult to sustain, because it is not only his sinlessness that differentiates Jesus from others but also the fact that he is believed to be both God and Man. The divinity of Jesus Christ means that he is worshipped, and, despite the fact that doctrinally it is heretical to separate his divinity from his humanity within his total identity, it is the divinity which tends to be accentuated in worship.

Human destiny lies in being transformed into the likeness of Jesus in some moral sense, and in a process that will be completed after death in the new order of heaven. Indeed the place of heaven and an after-life is quite crucial in the Christian doctrine of salvation, or soteriology as it is called. But here there is a possibility of a major difference of interpretation and opinion within Christianity. It hangs on whether one believes in an after-life or not.

HEAVEN AND EARTH

It has been traditional in Christianity to see human life as one phase of a total existence which will be perfected in heaven. One view sees heaven as the answer to the problem of why people suffer on earth. In heaven they will obtain the reward for what they suffered on earth. There is a Catholic view which presses the thought of an after-life in another direction, developing the idea of purgatory as a process through which God's grace operates on individuals to prepare them for the holiness of the divine presence.

But in more recent times some Christians have tended either to ignore the heavenly dimension or else to reject it when considering human nature and destiny. Though it is something of an over-generalisation, we might say that movements like Liberation, Black, and Feminist Theologies have tended to emphasise the vital importance of social justice in this world as the goal of Christian endeavour. This shows how varied ideas of human destiny can be.

Even so, for many Christians the hope of heaven is real. While they normally regard it as a 'place' where they worship God, they may also think in terms of heaven as a place to meet their dead relatives and friends – all as part of the process of their own coming to fulfilment as persons.

DEATH, DESTINY AND SALVATION

Even if life after death plays a very small part in the faith of some Christians, death remains a central issue for Christian faith itself because the death of Jesus is an absolutely crucial part of Christianity.

Christians view his death on the cross as a sacrifice for sin. Various interpretations explain this sacrifice in different ways. 'Substitutionary atonement' says that Jesus takes the place of guilty humans and dies in their place, and usually sees Jesus as the fulfilment of animal sacrifices for sin in the Old Testament. Some of the early Church Fathers regarded Jesus as a ransom paid to Satan, because Satan had gained authority over humanity after the Fall. Martin Luther in the Reformation and the Swede, Gustav Aulen, in the twentieth century saw the crucifixion as some sort of encounter between Christ and the devil.

The following quotation is from the end of Aulen's small but important book, *Christus Victor* (Aulen 1970). It expresses in a personal way the dynamic importance of the death of Christ for many believers.

> The Atonement is, above all, a movement of God to man, not in the first place a movement of man to God . . . God, the Infinite, accepts the

> lowliness of the Incarnation . . . We hear again the old realistic message of the conflict of God with the dark, hostile forces of evil, and His victory over them by the Divine self-sacrifice.
>
> (1931: 176)

In the 'exemplarist' view of the Atonement, Peter Abelard (1079–1142) saw the death of Jesus as the supreme example of the love of God, which triggered or stimulated a human response of repentance and responding love.

At around the same time, Anselm (1033–1109) interpreted atonement in a more legal or juridical theory, which made sense in the feudal society of his day. According to Anselm's theory human sin was a disgrace against the dignity of God. The price that was paid through the death of Jesus was paid not to Satan, but to God as a satisfaction of his outraged honour.

Types of salvation

The idea of salvation can also be usefully explored in religious studies from the perspective of sociology. Early this century (1922) Max Weber discussed the idea of salvation at some length in his *Sociology of Religion*. Arguing that 'every need for salvation is an expression of some distress' (1965: 107), he saw religion as one aspect of life among others that helped reduce distress. So, for example, he speaks of some poor and disprivileged groups as primarily needing a release from suffering: 'they do not always experience the need for salvation in a religious form' (1965: 108). What some rich people want is a sense of legitimacy – to feel that the good things they have are theirs by right – while intellectuals seeks a sense of meaning for the world. When Christianity is the official religion of a country, its theory of divine grace administered through the church can easily serve to provide just such a validation for the life lived by people in positions of power and responsibility.

In a very similar style to Max Weber, the English sociologist B.R. Wilson discussed salvation in religious sects. His classification or typology of sects is another interesting way of approaching human nature and destiny as far as religious people are concerned. Despite the fact that mainstream churches give an interpretation of life for millions of members of society, an important aspect of human nature in itself, there are many others who reject the dominant cultural interpretation and follow an alternative explanation of things. Wilson's sectarian types are, obviously, useful for describing such movements, but they also express some of the characteristics found in mainstream religions too. Wilson's basic argument is that each distinctive sect first describes evil and then proposes a remedy for it.

Conversionist groups say evil lies in the individual heart which needs to be converted through the Holy Spirit. *Revolutionists* say that the organisation of society is itself corrupt and can be changed only through a supernatural revolution brought about by God. *Reformists* also see evil in social structures, but think that they can bring about change through human endeavour. *Utopians* try to avoid the evil of society by setting up their own ideal social world apart from everyone else. Something similar is done by *Introversionists*, who try to live within holy groups of their own, surrounded by the wider evil society. *Manipulationists* try to pinpoint evil and cultivate a way of manipulating it so as to overcome it; secret knowledge or practices, known only to members, are the basis for manipulating negative and destructive tendencies. Finally, *Thaumaturgical* sects, a name from the Greek verb for wonder-working, specialise in dramatic acts such as healing or snake-handling to focus on evil and to show that its members have the means of overcoming it (Wilson 1970: 37 ff.).

Mood, human nature and salvation

One of Weber's many insights is that some groups cultivate a 'religious mood' as an 'instrument of salvation' (1965: 151). This is an important point for religious studies, since human nature is capable of being trained in many different ways. Weber emphasises the way different cultures and religious groups express their ideas and doctrines, and relate them to the active life of people. The way ideas are worked out in actions is related to the kind of mood which each group develops over time.

One aspect of human nature that is deeply involved in theories of human destiny is music. This might seem a strange thing to say, but it is important for religious studies.

Human beings not only have the capacity to speak and to enjoy the power of words, but also to sing and to be inspired by the power of music. This must not be taken for granted. In practice, most Christian traditions use music in worship. The Greek Orthodox forbid musical instruments in worship but sing or chant the largest part of the liturgy. Catholic and Protestant traditions were the central sources of musical creativity for a thousand years in Europe, and, through missionary work and emigration, also in many other parts of the world.

Doctrinal ideas about God, humanity, life, and death have all been expressed poetically in hymns, and sung. Such singing in worship has helped millions to grasp the hope of divine help and of an eternal dimension to life. Sometimes music on its own helps inspire people to transcend the ordinary levels of existence in which they normally live. Religious music exists in many forms, from the military style of Salvation Army bands to the mystical chanting of monks. In popular thought, even the angels are said to play harps in heaven. In practical terms, music has the effect of uniting people together as a group and also of giving a sense of unity to individuals within themselves. This brings us to the question of what makes up a human being?

Human nature: soul and/or body

Two broad kinds of explanation of human nature are found in Christianity. Perhaps the one that has been, and continues to be, dominant divides human beings into body and soul, or into body, soul and spirit, as in 1 Thess. 5: 23. This internal division has a long history and was widespread in ancient Greek thought. In Plato, for example, the soul is a prisoner within the body set free only by death. Much of this has had an influence on Christianity.

But the other tradition, with its roots in Jewish thought, sees people as a single physical entity. Though in a rather metaphorical way the body may be said to possess the breath of life, human nature remains a physical thing that ceases existence at death. The idea of the resurrection of the body relates to this view, and sees any future life after death as dependent upon a new creation and a definite act of God, rather than upon some immortal soul passing on its way from earth to heaven.

Much modern Christian thinking prefers this unified approach to the individual, and uses it to talk of salvation as wholeness of the entire person rather than as the salvation of the soul. The ethical issue of abortion is one practical area where the question of what constitutes human nature is important. To believe that the soul comes to the growing embryo at some specific point of development, defines human nature in terms of possessing a soul. But if human nature is defined in terms of the ongoing development of the body and its personality through relationships with other people, then no single moment stamps the human animal as a human being.

Human nature: society and individual

One final and radically important aspect of defining human nature from a Christian perspective concerns society. From its Jewish background, Christianity took the idea of a community of people existing in a covenant relationship with God. To this it added the belief that, in Jesus Christ, God had participated in human life and opened the boundaries of the covenant to include all people. The church exists as a kind of symbol of this total human group linked to God.

One feature of what is called 'theological anthropology', or the doctrine of human nature, is that Christianity sees individuals as members of a group, whether a covenant community, a family, or the church. While individuals are important, their prime place is within a community. The New Testament idea of a community existing as the 'body of Christ', with everyone linked in to others through the varied gifts, duties and responsibilities of each, is basic to the Christian view of human nature and destiny (Rom. 12: 4).

In theological terms, the social nature of human life is sometimes seen as a reflection of the Holy Trinity as a group of 'persons' interacting with each other. This 'social' model of the Trinity is one way of seeing humanity made in the image of God, with a capacity for relationship with others, and, even more than that, a necessity of relationship with others. Following this line of thought, human nature is essentially social, and human destiny is to be in developing relationships with other humans and with God.

FAITH, LOVE AND HOPE

It is as the collective body of Christ that Christians live by faith in God and seek to express the love of God to all through their own ethical living. Faith and love express two aspects of life that are intrinsic to Christian values. Hope is a third 'theological virtue' that characterises a Christian understanding of human nature (1 Cor. 13: 13). Hope lies in the will and purpose of God for humanity. Together faith, hope and love are opposed to unbelief, despair and egoism, in the total life of Christians.

Destiny's goal

We began this chapter by focusing on creation. We said that Christian wonder at the world's complexity and at the very fact of its existence came to centre on the doctrine of creation. In an interesting way this stress on God's act of making the universe draws attention away from God's more immediate nature. This is a rather subtle but important point. The doctrine of creation looks at an empirical and factual world of things; it asks Christians to see God through and behind the creation. The doctrine of creation comes to be one of the standard working doctrines of daily Christian life.

We have also seen that the greater part of the Christian tradition asserts that human existence does not end with death. Human destiny is said to come to its true goal in a relationship with God after death. And it is here that a shift of focus takes place, moving away from the doctrine of creation to the nature of God in a more direct way. Instead of revelation through the medium of creation there is a direct knowledge of God. Human destiny shifts from the creation to the Creator.

FURTHER READING

Anselm, Saint. *Cur Deus Homo*.

Aulen, G. (1970) *Christus Victor*, London, SPCK (first published in 1931).

Casey, M. (1991) *From Jewish Prophet to Gentile God*, Cambridge, James Clarke.

Davies, D.J. (1991) *F.B. Jevons: An Evolutionary Realist*, New York, Mellen Press.

Hartshorne, C.S. (1967) *A Natural Theology for our Time*, Illinois, Open Court.

Jevons, F.B. (1896) *Introduction to the History of Religion*, London, Methuen.

—— (1906) *Religion in Evolution*, London, Methuen.

Lewis, I.M. (1986) *Religion in Context*, Cambridge, Cambridge University Press.

Ogden, S.M. (1979) *Faith and Freedom*, Nashville, Abingdon.

Pittinger, N. (1967) *God in Process*, London, SCM.

Russell, J.B. (1977) *The Devil*, New York, New American Library.

Skultans, V. (1974) *Intimacy and Distance*, London, Routledge.

Teilhard de Chardin, P. (1965) *Hymn of the Universe*, London, Collins.

Thornton, L.S. (1928) *The Incarnate Lord*, London, Longman.

—— (1950) *Revelation and the Modern World*, Westminster, Dacre Press.

Tillich, P. (1953) *Systematic Theology*, London, Nesbit.

Weber, M. (1965) *The Sociology of Religion*, London, Methuen (first published in German in 1922).

Whitehead, A. (1926) *Religion in the Making*.

Wilson, B.R. (1970) *Religious Sects*, New York, World University Press.

3. Hinduism

Anantanand Rambachan

The value of human existence

Birth as a human being is considered to be a rare privilege in the Hindu understanding. Among the various species of life, the human being exhibits an unrivalled capacity for choice in action and the ability for acquiring knowledge. The human being is capable, not only of gathering empirical information about the world, but also of speculating and wondering about the ultimate meaning and purpose, if any, of existence. The concern and quest for meaning is, as far as we know, unique to the human species. Because of this potential for ascertaining life's meaning and achieving fullness of existence, Hindu scriptural texts repeatedly remind us of the opportunities of human existence.

The Hindi poet, Tulasidas (c. 1532–1623), in the extremely influential text, the *Rāmacaritamānas* (commonly referred to as the *Rāmāyaṇa*), extols the significance of human existence.

> It is a great and good fortune that you have secured a human body, which – as all the scriptures declare – is difficult even for heavenly beings to attain. It is a tabernacle suitable for spiritual discipline and the gateway to liberation.
>
> (pp. 720–1)

While praising the possibility offered by human existence for the attainment of liberation (*mokṣa*), the Hindu scriptures also lament the fact that few avail themselves of this opportunity. 'Those born as human beings', says Tulasidas, 'who indulge only in the limited delights of the senses, are fools who would choose poison in exchange for nectar'. In *Bhagavadgītā* 7: 3, Kṛṣna similarly laments that only one person, among many thousands, strives for liberation. The philosopher and theologian, Śaṃkara, in his famous poem, *Vivekacūḍāmaṇi* (4–5), contends that one who is fortunate to be born as a human being and who does not make appropriate efforts for liberation commits suicide by clinging on to things that have no ultimate value. 'What greater fool is there', asks Śaṃkara, 'than the person who having obtained a human body, neglects to achieve the real end of this life?'

The four goals

While the Hindu tradition upholds liberation (*mokṣa*) as life's ultimate end and, in one sense, only goal, it has also accepted the legitimacy of other subsidiary goals in the scheme of human existence. In most cases, according to the Hindu viewpoint, the necessity and desire for *mokṣa* are appreciated only after the experience of these subsidiary goals and their limitations. What are these auxiliary ends and how are they limited?

The various legitimate ends (*puruṣārthas*) which a human being is capable of pursuing and achieving have been classified by Hinduism under four headings. The first of these is *kāma*, or pleasure. *Kāma* includes sensual as well as aesthetic enjoyment. Sculpture, music and dance flourished with the blessings of Hinduism, and Hindus love to celebrate life through these forms. The Hindu recognition of *kāma* as a valid human pursuit challenges the common characterisation of this tradition as being life-negating and other-worldly. While it is indeed true that Hinduism does not uphold *kāma* as life's highest value, it has not been condemned as intrinsically evil. As long as the individual has the maturity and good sense to be moderate in indulgence and to observe standard rules of morality (*dharma*), he or she has the approval of Hinduism to fulfil the urge for pleasure. The fundamental role of *dharma* to be observed is the avoidance of injury, distress and suffering to others.

Kāma, however, is dependent for its realisation and expression on the gain of *artha* (worldly success). The term *artha* is very broad in its application and, while including wealth, it also encompasses success, power and prestige. By acknowledging *artha*, Hinduism recognises the need of every human being for access to those material necessities which make life possible and comfortable, and which enable one to fulfil social obligations and duties. While historically approving the voluntary renunciation of material possessions in order to seek liberation, Hinduism has never given its blessing to involuntary poverty and material deprivation. T.W. Organ was correct when he wrote that the 'impoverished state of both the private and public sectors of the Indian economy should not be interpreted to mean that Hinduism has blessed poverty, in spite of the words and actions of no less honored leaders than Mahatma Gandhi and Vinoba Bhave' (Organ 1970: 125).

While freely giving its approval to the pursuit of *kāma* and *artha*, the Hindu scriptures continuously call our attention to the limitations of these twin ends. We are told that these, although valid, will never fully satisfy our deepest needs, and their attainment will still leave us incomplete. The reasons afforded are many. The gains of pleasure and worldly success are transient, leaving us hopelessly addicted to their momentary gratifications. This is the insight of *Bhagavadgītā* 5: 22.

> Whatever pleasures are born out of contact [between the mind, senses and objects], are sources of sorrow, since they have a beginning and an end. O son of Kuntī [Arjuna], a wise person does not indulge in these.

Ultimately, in death, we leave wealth and worldly success behind.

There are other reasons, however, why *kāma* and *artha* leave us unsatisfied. Wealth, fame and power are exclusive and, therefore, competitive and risky (Smith 1958: 19–20). These are assets which diminish when they are shared. One lives in uncertainty as to whether one's rivals will soon gain the advantage, and hence one suffers from inadequacy and uncertainty. 'The idea of a nation', writes Smith, 'in which everyone is famous is a contradiction in terms; if power were distributed equally no one would be powerful in the sense in which we customarily use the word. Fame consists in standing out from one's fellows and power is control over them. From the competitiveness of these values to their riskiness is one short step.'

The pursuit of *kāma* and *artha* does not distinguish us as a unique species of living beings. Other forms of life, in different degrees, have material needs and reflect the capacity for pleasure. It is the third end of human existence, *dharma*, which, in the first instance, distinguishes us as human beings.

Dharma is a very rich and multi-faceted concept, and therefore difficult to define. It is derived from the Sanskrit root *dhṛ*, meaning to support or to sustain, and can be partly equated with duty, morality and virtue. The goal of *dharma* emphasises the social context in which we exist and in which we strive for *artha* and *kāma*, and the need to regulate these pursuits in the interests of the whole. *Dharma*, in other words, establishes the boundaries for *kāma* and *artha*. The personal attainment of worldly success and enjoyment by inflicting pain and suffering on others, or by denying them the right freely to pursue these ends, is opposed to *dharma*. *Dharma* is the goal in Hinduism which presupposes the special human capacity for concern and responsiveness to the needs and interests of others. We are the only animal species with the ability to make conscious moral choices in relation to our wealth- and pleasure-oriented activities. Being human requires that we continuously exercise this choice.

The concept of *dharma* also includes particular duties and obligations to be followed by members of the four Hindu *varṇa*s (social groups) and by persons in the four stages (*āśrama*s) of life. The term *varṇāśrāma dharma* refers to duties as related to caste and stage in life.[1] In the *Bhagavadgītā* 2: 31–7, Kṛṣna points out to Arjuna the necessity of being faithful to his duty as a member of the warrior (*kṣatriya*) caste in order to convince him to engage in battle against his unjust cousins. Failure to engage in battle will be an abnegation of duty (*svadharma*), with a consequent loss of honour.

High value, therefore, is placed on *dharma*, and on meeting the difficulties of living up to its demands. But, as with *kāma* and *artha*, it is not considered to be the highest end of human existence. In other words, a life which consisted of the search for pleasure and worldly success within the boundaries of *dharma* would still not exhaust the human potential. Even society, the object of *dharma*, is, after all, limited. 'Even when extended through history,' writes Huston Smith, 'the human community, as long as it stands alone remains both finite and tragic; tragic not only in the sense that it must eventually come to an end, but also in its inflexible resistance to perfection. The final want of man must lie elsewhere' (Smith 1958: 24–5). The term *mokṣa*, is the fulfilment of human want and, in the Hindu view, our highest goal.

We do not, however, come to the discovery of our need for *mokṣa* very easily. It is the rarest of all human desires and is discovered only when we have experienced or reflected on the frustrations and limitations of *kāma* and *artha*, and long for a fullness which is not transient. It is the close examination and analysis of the limitations of our many pursuits and their inability to lead us to fullness which bring us to the *mokṣa*-quest.

Mokṣa liberates us not only from the sense of want, but also from the repetitive cycle of birth and death (*saṃsāra*) to which we are subject. So long as we remain content with the finite gains and results of *artha* and *kāma*, we will continue to be caught in the chain of births and deaths. This cycle is seen as being perpetuated entirely by the forces of our desires, and the actions and results which they entail. The meaning of *mokṣa* will not be appreciated unless the realities of rebirth and *karma* are understood: for Hindus, it is ignorance (*avidyā*) at least as much as fault or sin which impedes progress towards *mokṣa*. What, then, do rebirth and *karma* mean?

Rebirth and *karma*

All the traditions of Hinduism hold the doctrine of the rebirth of the individual after death. The term used to describe this process is *punarjanma*, which literally means 'birth after death'. The basic belief is that we do not cease to exist at the end of this current life, but that we are born again, in this or some other world (*loka*), with a new physical body. Like the universe itself, which is viewed in Hinduism as always existing, but which goes through cycles of manifestation and dissolution, individual beings also have an existence that is without beginning. Under the impulse of desires (*kāma*) of various kinds, a variety of actions (*karma*) are performed and these produce results (*karmaphala*) which must be experienced by the performer of the action. The necessity to experience the consequences of one's actions requires embodiment in some form or another, during which result-producing actions continue to be performed – and so the cycle of birth and death, referred to as *saṃsāra*, endures.

For the purpose of appreciating the doctrine of *punarjanma*, we must understand that the true being or identity of the human person, in the Hindu view, is the self (*ātman*). It is the changeless basis and unifying reality of all other changing components of the human personality. It is described in *Bhagavadgītā* 2: 20 as being free from birth and death, changeless and eternal. The *ātman* is clothed with, though not limited by, the psychophysical components of the individual personality, and these are described as consisting of three bodies, constituting, as it were, the vehicle of the self (*VC*: 87–109).

The outermost body or sheath is the physical body, referred to as the gross body (*sthūla śarīra*). It is so called because it is composed of matter in the same form as the visible universe and can be perceived and experienced through the sense organs. *Bhagavadgītā* 5: 13 likens the physical body to a city of nine gates (*navadvāre pure*) in which dwells the master or *ātman*. The nine gates referred to are the two eyes, the two ears, the two nostrils, the mouth, and the organs of excretion. The gross body is regarded as being different from the self, for whom it is an object of knowledge and an instrument of action.

Different from the gross body is the subtle body (*sūkṣma śarīra*), so called because it is composed of matter in a subtle or uncompounded form.[2] Its components include all thinking and decision-making faculties.[3] The subtle body is also different from the self, for whom it is an object and instrument of knowledge. It is considered to be the repository of all our tendencies (*vāsanās*), good and evil.

The third body, or sheath, is the causal body (*kārana śarīra*). It expresses itself most prominently in the state of deep sleep, when all mental, emotional and intellectual activities become dormant and unmanifest. From this latent or causal condition, they again emerge to express themselves in experiences of waking and dreaming. The term 'causal' is justified since the gross and subtle bodies are absorbed, as it were, into the causal body at the time of deep sleep, and from it they again emerge (*VC*: 120–1). The causal body is regarded as being other than the *ātman*, to whom it is also related as an object. Even as one is aware of one's physical body and mental states, one is also aware of the ignorance of the deep sleep state, and this direct knowledge is expressed in the waking affirmation, 'I slept happily; I did not know anything'. I know, in other words, that I did not know anything.

The event of death marks the disintegration of the gross body. The individual being (*jīva*), clothed with the subtle and causal bodies, seeks a new physical form to express its peculiar inclinations and to experience the results of previous actions. The self is associated with its gross and causal bodies until the attainment of *mokṣa*, when, freed from these, it is no longer subject to *saṃsāra* (*BSBS*: IV. ii. 8–11).

The movement from death to rebirth has been strikingly compared in the *Bhagavadgītā* (2: 26) to a change of clothing:

> Just as a person casts off worn-out garments and puts on others that are new, even so does the embodied soul cast off worn-out bodies and take on others that are new.

This suggestive analogy makes a number of important points about the rebirth process. First, even as a suit of clothing is not identical with the wearer, similarly the gross body, likened here to worn-out garments, is not the true being or identity of the human person. Secondly, there is a similarity of continuity. When a worn-out suit of clothing is cast off, the wearer continues to be. Similarly, with the disintegration of the gross body in death, the indweller – that is the *ātman* – continues to be. The third point brings us to the relationship between the cycle of birth and death and the doctrine of *karma*. A suit of clothing is cast off when it no longer serves the purpose for which it was worn. Similarly, the gross body is dropped when it has fulfilled the purpose for which it came into existence. Each life-experience is conditioned by those that preceded it. The gross body, as a vital and necessary component in any particular birth, is also conditioned by prior births. It is the instrument through which diverse experience of pleasure (*sukha*) and pain (*duḥkha*), consistent with past attitudes and actions, is gained. Its reason or justification for existence is attained when these experiences are realised and, like a suit of worn clothing, it is shed.

Saṃsāra, therefore, is by no means conceived by Hindus to be a haphazard process, but one governed by the law of action and reaction (*karma*). Hinduism envisages the universe as a moral stage where 'all living beings get the dress and part that befit them and are to act well to deserve well in the future' (Chatterjee and Datta 1968: 18). The term *karma* literally means action, but it also includes the subtle forces which are understood to be generated by all voluntary actions, and which are seen as capable of producing results in the future. The doctrine, or law, of *karma* is basically an extension into the moral sphere of the physical law of causation. It implies that all moral actions are as potent as physical ones, and are capable of producing appropriate results in the future.

Every action – physical, verbal or mental – has an immediate effect, but it also creates an impression on the subtle body which bears appropriate fruit in due course. The result depends, of course, on the nature and quality of the action. The *Bṛhadāraṇyaka Upaniṣad* (4. 4. 5) succinctly expresses this point:

> According as one acts, according as one conducts oneself, so does one become. The doer of good becomes good. The doer of evil becomes evil. One becomes virtuous by virtuous action, bad by bad action.

It will not, of course, surprise the reader to note that Hindus resist the equation of the doctrine of *karma* with fatalism and predestination. The doctrine is sometimes understood to be denying freedom of will and choice for the human being. It is argued that we lose all initiative and responsibility for actions if our experiences in the present life are determined by our actions in the past.

From the Hindu standpoint, however, the law of *karma* emphasises free-will and insists upon moral responsibility. If in my present life I am experiencing the results and consequences of past actions, this is only because I was responsible for those actions. The important point, of course, is that if I have influenced my present condition by my past behaviour, there is no reason why I should not be able to shape my future through my present conduct. The law of *karma* stipulates that certain kinds of actions will produce certain results, but this does not necessarily paralyse the human will. On the contrary, it places responsibility squarely on my shoulders, since it does not propose a power outside myself which is responsible for my individual and collective destiny (Chatterjee 1970: 82–100).

From the Hindu standpoint, the basic urge of all human beings is the desire for fullness (*ānanda*). There is an inner inadequacy and incompleteness which yearns for fulfilment and which expresses itself in multifarious desires. Smith wrote of it as a desire for joy, 'a resolution of feelings in which the basic themes are the opposite of frustration, futility and boredom' (Smith 1958: 26). In the *Chāndogya Upaniṣad* (VII 1.2–3), we are given the example of Nārada, who comes to his teacher enumerating all the branches of knowledge which he has mastered. Among these are the Veda, grammar, mathematics, ethics, logic, philosophy, physical science and the science of war. Yet, declares Nārada, 'I am in sorrow, please make me pass beyond sorrow'. Nārada's sorrow is the pain of an inward incompleteness which all these forms of learning could not resolve.

This basic human desire for fullness expresses itself outwardly in changing desires for objects of pleasure (*kāma*) and various forms of worldly success (*artha*). The fulfilment of any one of these desires allows one temporarily to own oneself to be a full person, but, very soon, that insufficiency is experienced once more and new desires are entertained. Like a person fighting a raging fire by pouring fresh fuel into the flames, the satisfaction of any number of limited desires does not lead to freedom from desire. Like Naciketas in the *Kaṭha Upaniṣad*, we will discover that the human being cannot be satisfied with material gains and accomplishments.

The Non-dualist view: Śaṃkara

In the vision of Hinduism, and particularly according to the tradition of *Advaita Vedānta* (Non-dualism) systematised by Śaṃkara (c. 788–820), we fail to accomplish the fullness which we seek because the very seeking itself is based on an acceptance of the false premise that we are, in reality, incomplete and insufficient. We search for fullness without, in the first place, asking the question, 'Who am I?' If we inquired properly into this question we would indeed discover that we are already the full beings which we seek to be.

The reason we do not inquire, according to most of the traditions of Hinduism, is that we are all the victims of a beginningless ignorance (*avidyā*). This ignorance, though not limited to, is precisely about, ourselves. It is regarded as basic because our conduct and responses to others and to our environment are, in large measure, determined by our understanding and image of ourselves. Hinduism has a generally optimistic view about the goodness of human nature. The *Aitareya Upaniṣad* (1. 2. 3), for example, declares the human being to be well-formed and truly fit for righteous action. Attitudes and patterns of conduct which are harmful to oneself and to others are seen as having their causes not in any intrinsic defect in human nature but in false knowledge. The gain of valid knowledge not only removes ignorance, but is expected also to correct erroneous values and conduct.

A popular story is employed by Hindu teachers of the *Advaita Vedānta* tradition to explain the nature of our ignorance and the overcoming of it by knowledge. Ten disciples were on their way to a pilgrimage site when they encountered a river in flood. In the absence of a boat, they decided to swim across the river. On reaching the opposite shore, the leader took a count to ensure that everyone was safe. To his dismay, one seemed to be missing. Every other member of the group did likewise, but ended up with the same result. They were all in deep grief after concluding that the tenth person had drowned. A passer-by, attracted by their loud lamentations, inquired about their problem. After patiently listening and observing, he assured them that the tenth person was indeed available and requested the leader to count again. When the disciple stopped at nine and looked bewildered, the stranger smilingly said, 'You are the tenth person!' The error was immediately appreciated. Each had left himself out from his count.

As a consequence of ignorance, according to Śaṃkara, we identify ourselves with the qualities of our limited gross and subtle bodies and superimpose upon the true self the characteristics of these.

> For instance, a man superimposes the attributes of external things on his self, if he thinks himself as sound or unsound when his wife, son, etc., are sound or unsound; similarly, he superimposes the attributes of his body on his self, if he thinks himself fat, lean, fair, standing, going or jumping; similarly he superimposes the attributes of the senses on the self when he regards himself as dumb or one-eyed, impotent, deaf or blind; similarly he superimposes on his own self the attributes of the internal organ like desire, resolve, doubt and determination, etc. In this way, after superimposing the denotations of the concept of 'I' on the inner self that is the witness of its entire activities, and vice-versa, one superimposes that inner self, the witness of all, on the internal organ etc.
>
> (*BSBS*, intro.)

The *ātman*, which is different from all psychophysical processes, is wrongly identified with the limited characteristics of these, and regarded as subject to birth and death, change and incompleteness. One of Śaṃkara's principal arguments for the distinction of the *ātman* from the body and mind is that, even as one is aware of external objects, one is aware of bodily and mental processes. The relationship with these is that of knower and known. The *ātman*, which witnesses all bodily and mental changes, is itself free from all change. It remains the same in all periods of time and is regarded, therefore, as *sat* (eternal). Awareness or consciousness is intrinsic to the *ātman*, whereas everything else is inert. For this reason, the *ātman* is said to be self-luminous. Śaṃkara argues that everyone immediately knows that he or she *is*, and one does not require proof of one's existence (*BSBS*, intro.). Every other object, however, including the body and mind, is illumined and revealed by the self-luminous *ātman*. The nature of the *ātman* as awareness and, indeed, according to Śaṃkara, as the only conscious principle in the whole of existence, is indicated by the word, *cit*. Finally, the *ātman* is said to be *ananta* or *ānanda*, which indicates its fullness and freedom from limitations of all kinds as well as its nature as the basis and source of all joy.

The Sanskrit expression *sat–cit–ānanda* (reality–awareness–joy) describes the nature of the *ātman*.[4] Because the *ātman* is free from all limitations, therefore, it is identical, for Śaṃkara, with *brahman* – the infinite. In fact, for Śaṃkara, the terms *ātman* and *brahman* are interchangeable. The word *ātman* is used to describe the limitless self from an individual standpoint, while the word *brahman* is used for the self in its cosmic and universal nature as the reality of all existence. *Ātman* and *brahman*, in other words, are not two different realities, but rather terms describing one and the same reality.

For Śaṃkara, the great sentence (*mahāvākya*) of the *Chāndogya Upaniṣad*, '*Tat Tvam Asi*' (That Thou Art), teaches the unequivocal identity of *ātman* and *brahman*.[5] This sentence, contends Śaṃkara, does not ask us to look upon the *ātman* as if it were *brahman*, but asserts a definite identity. It is also not to be conceived figuratively (*gauṇa*) as in the sentence, 'You are a lion', nor as a mere praise of the student, Śvetaketu. The latter is not an object of worship in the discussion and it is no praise to *brahman* to be identified with Śvetaketu.

Subject to ignorance, like the tenth person, we do not realise that we are the fullness which we seek in erroneous ways. For Śaṃkara, the *Upaniṣads* (the last section of the Veda, also referred to as the *Vedānta*), constitute a valid means of knowledge in the form of words (*śabda-pramāṇa*) for eliminating ignorance and correcting our knowledge of the self (Rambachan 1991). The teacher (*guru*) has an indispensable function as someone who has mastered the wisdom of the scripture and who is established in the knowledge of the self. By listening carefully to the words of the texts as unfolded by the teacher (*śravaṇa*), by the application of reason and analysis to remove doubts (*manana*), and by a continuous contemplation (*nididhyāsana*) on the nature of the *ātman* to eliminate false values and attitudes, one becomes established in the knowledge of the self. Spiritual disciplines, including the practical methods of *yoga*, are helpful to the extent that they steady and purify the mind. These serve, therefore, only as indirect aids for the attainment of *mokṣa*. Since the self is always available, but misunderstood, knowledge is the direct means to liberation.

For Śaṃkara, *mokṣa* is synonymous with the gain of self-knowledge, since the fundamental problem is one of ignorance. He subscribes, therefore, to the doctrine of liberation in life (*jīvan-mukti*), and not as a post-mortem accomplishment. The liberated person continues in mortal existence only as long as the *karma*, which has brought the particular body into being, endures. Such *karma* may be compared to an arrow which is released from a bow. Even if the archer changes his or her mind, the released arrow must travel to its destination. The exhaustion of *karma* results in liberation from the body (*videha mukti*) and freedom from *saṃsāra*.

Such liberation, it must be emphasised, is not the attainment of immortal existence in some other world. Being identical with the infinite self, it defies definition.

> Sankara declares in many passages that the nature of liberation is a state of oneness with *brahman*, and even as the latter is lifted above all categories of experience, so the state of *mokṣa* cannot be described in terms of our knowledge. Since the latter deals with distinctions of space and time, cause and effect, persons and things, action and suffering, it is said that none of these distinctions applies to the state of freedom. It cannot be said that the liberated live in the geographical area called *svarga* or *brahmaloka*; nor can it be said that they last for endless time.
>
> (Radhakrishnan 1977, vol. 2: 639–40)

For Śaṃkara, then, the attainment of *brahman* through knowledge (*jñāna*) is identical with liberation. *Brahman*, as we have seen, is not different from one's own self. It has the highest value because it is that which is ultimately real. Śaṃkara, however, does not equate *brahman* with the world, since *brahman* in its transcendental nature far exceeds the universe, and since the universe has characteristics of change, insentience and limitations which are opposed to the nature of *brahman* (Rambachan 1989: 287–97). As *brahman* is the efficient cause and the material basis of the universe, the latter does not exist apart from *brahman*. The infinite *brahman* underlies and runs through all finite effects and these cannot be considered as standing outside of *brahman*.

Śaṃkara neither equates *brahman* with the world, nor asserts that the world possesses a reality which is independent of *brahman*. Avoiding both positions, the *Advaita* tradition asserts that the world, in its relationship to *brahman*, is a mystery and is indefinable (*anirvacanīya*). Without undergoing any change or losing anything of itself, *brahman* is both cause and source of the world. We may view the world as the mysterious manifestation of *brahman*. It is not the infinite plus something else, but the infinite mysteriously appearing as the finite. The nature of *brahman*, it must be remembered, is non-dual.

The Qualified Non-dualist view: Rāmānuja

Śaṃkara's understanding of human nature and destiny has had a deep and wide influence on Hinduism, but there are other influential interpretations. Prominent among these is the *Viśiṣṭadvaita* (Qualified Non-dualism) system promulgated by the south Indian theologian, Rāmānuja (traditionally 1017–1137).

Rāmānuja's differences with Śaṃkara on human nature and destiny are all fundamentally related to their different understandings of the nature of *brahman*. Rāmānuja shares with Śaṃkara the view that *brahman* is the only reality. There is, in other words, no other reality outside or independent of *brahman*. However, for Rāmānuja, *brahman*, or God, is internally diverse and complex (*viśiṣṭa*). The all-inclusive *brahman* contains within itself a real diversity, consisting of unconscious matter (*acit*) and conscious selves (*cit*). The term *viśiṣṭādvaita* becomes justified, since the one (*advaita*) *brahman* is qualified (*viśiṣṭa*) by an internal diversity consisting of matter and souls.

Unlike Śaṃkara, who argues for the identity of the self in all beings, Rāmānuja admits that there is a plurality of selves distinct from each other. A central concern of Rāmānuja is the clarification of the relationship existing between God, matter and souls. He attempts his clarification by employing the body–soul analogy. Matter and souls are described by him as constituting the body of God. While our souls are souls in relation to our body, in relation to God our soul becomes part of God's body, and God ought to be seen as the soul of all souls and of matter. The relation between God and the matter and souls which make up God's body, is not identity, but inseparability (*apṛthak-siddhi*). In Rāmānuja's view, a body is that which is utilised and supported by a conscious entity for its own purpose, and which is under the control of that entity.

> Any substance which a sentient soul is capable of completely controlling and supporting for its own purposes, and which stands to the soul in an entirely subordinate relation, is the body of that soul . . . In that sense, then, all sentient and non-sentient beings together constitute the body of the Supreme Person, for they are completely controlled and supported by him for his own ends, and are absolutely subordinate to him.
>
> (*VCR*, II. 1. 9)

Brahman is the support (*ādhāra*), controller (*niyantā*) and principal (*śeṣin*), while the individual souls and matter are supported (*dhārya*), controlled (*niyāmya*) and the means (*śeṣa*). Though dependent and inseparable from *brahman*, souls and matter are real.

For Rāmānuja, unlike Śaṃkara, *brahman* is not an indeterminate (*nirguṇa*) and indefinable reality, but possessed of infinitely good qualities. Among these are limitless knowledge and bliss. God is the creator, sustainer and destroyer of the world, which is brought forth from the matter that is co-existent with and within God. Even when the world is withdrawn into God, there remains within God undifferentiated matter as well as souls, since both are eternal.

The bondage of the soul, for Rāmānuja, is due to ignorance and *karma*. Ignorant of its true nature as a spiritual substance related to God as part, the soul identifies itself with the body and mind, from which it is different, and becomes subject to desires of various kinds. Liberation is attained through a harmonious combination of work (*karma*), knowledge (*jñāna*) and devotion (*bhakti*). By work, Rāmānuja means the diligent performance of rituals which are enjoyed in the first sections of the Veda. The performance of these rituals with the motive only of pleasing God and without a desire for reward of any kind destroys the accumulated effects of past actions. One also realises, however, that rituals of this kind cannot lead directly to *mokṣa*. The aspirant then moves on to the study of the last sections of the Veda, that is the *Upaniṣads*. From this study, one comes to an understanding of the nature of the soul and its true relationship to God. One learns that the soul is not identical with the body and mind, but is related to God as part to whole, and entirely dependent on God.

This understanding of one's dependence on God leads to an acknowledgement of God as the only object worthy of adoration, and to a loving and unbroken remembrance of God (*dhruvā smṛtiḥ*). This attitude of intense love and self-surrender (*prapatti*) towards God, when combined with the performance of obligatory rituals, pleases God whose grace (*prasāda*) brings about the final liberation of the soul (*VCR*, I. 1. 1). Through grace, ignorance and *karma* are destroyed and the soul comes into immediate knowledge of God. While Śaṃkara acknowledges the significance of divine grace, Rāmānuja obviously attributes to it a central and indispensable role for liberation.

For Rāmānuja, unlike Śaṃkara, liberation is not the discovery by the soul of its identity with *brahman*. The soul realises its nature as a part of God's body, but retains its individuality and distinctiveness from God and other souls.

> For scriptural and *smṛti* texts alike declare that the released soul stands to the highest Self in relation of fellowship, equality, equality of attributes, and all this implies a consciousness of separation.
>
> (*VCR*, IV. 4. 4)

Unlike God, who is all-pervasive, the soul is atomic in size; also it does not share rulership of the world with God.

The most visible inheritors, in the western world, of the theology of Rāmānuja are the members of ISKON (the International Society for Krishna Consciousness), an organisation founded in the United States in 1966 by A.C. Bhaktivedanta Swami Prabhupada. Drawing generally from the tradition of Vaiṣṇavism, and more specifically from the disciplic succession initiated by the Bengali devotee, Caitanya (1485–1533), the movement emphasises that the goal of human existence is the discovery of oneself to be part and parcel of God, and to be engaged in the loving service of God. The proponents of *Advaita* were continuously censured by Prabhupada for their characterisation of ultimate reality as impersonal, and for denying all distinctions in the liberated state. Since the name of God is not different from God, the recommended technique for cultivating devotion and expressing devotional service is the chanting of the sacred mantra, '*Hare Kṛṣṇa, Hare Kṛṣṇa, Kṛṣṇa Kṛṣṇa, Hare Hare/ Hare Rāma, Hare Rāma, Rāma Rāma, Hare Hare*'.[6]

The Dualist view: Madhva

Śaṃkara, as we have seen, spoke of the relationship between the self and ultimate reality as one of identity. Rāmānuja, on the other hand, rejected identity and described the relationship as one of inseparability. Madhvāchārya (c. 1238–1317), a bitter opponent of Śaṃkara's views, went a step further and argued for an unqualified dualism (*dvaita*).

For Madhva, like Rāmānuja, there are three real and eternal entities. These are God, souls and matter. These three are distinct and different, and Madhva qualifies these differences as being fivefold:

1. God is distinct from souls,
2. God is distinct from non-living matter,
3. each soul is distinct from another,
4. souls are distinct from matter,
5. matter particles, when separated, are distinct from one another.

God, according to Madhva, is the only independent reality. Souls and matter are subordinate to, and dependent on, God. God, whose nature is existence, knowledge and bliss, possesses a perfect nature and infinitely good qualities. God creates, sustains and destroys the world. Endowed with a supernatural body, God is transcendent. As the inner controller of all souls (*antaryāmin*), however, God is also immanent. God can incarnate at will, without becoming, in any way, limited. Madhva identifies God with Viṣṇu, and describes him as having the goddess Lakṣmī as his eternal companion. Like God, Lakṣmī is free from ignorance and bondage.

She is the personification of his creative power and, through her, he creates, sustains and destroys the universe.

Unlike matter which is inert, souls are conscious and blissful by nature. Like Rāmānuja, Madhva describes the souls as being atomic in size. Due to the force of past *karma*, souls are entangled with material bodies and subject to the cycle of births and deaths. Madhva classifies souls into those that are eternally free (*nitya*), like Lakṣmī, those that have freed themselves from bondage (*mukta*), and those that are bound (*baddha*). Among the latter, there are some souls who are eligible for release, but others who will never gain release from the experience of *saṃsāra*. Madhva's doctrine of an eternal *saṃsāra* is unique among teachers of Hinduism.

The liberation of the individual is neither through knowledge nor through works, but solely through the grace of God (*Īśvara-praśāda*). Madhva's understanding of divine grace reminded Radhakrishnan of the Augustinian view in Christianity.

> A man can never desire to be saved. It is only through grace that he can be redeemed. God is not forced by any consideration of merit. He simply elects some for salvation and others for the opposite state. The divine will sets men free or casts them into bondage. But the Hindu tradition does not allow Madhva to hold that God's choice is arbitrary, unconditioned and groundless. Though in a sense the states of the soul are brought about by *brahman*, it is also admitted that the grace of the Lord is proportioned to the intensity of our devotion.

(Radhakrishnan 1977, vol. 2: 747–8)

While Rāmānuja describes the liberated soul as similar to God in some respects, Madhva is concerned to stress the differences between God and the liberated soul. Consistent with his theology of difference, he emphasises the distinctions in the experience of liberation, even for the emancipated soul. At the lowest level, the soul gains entry into the heavenly abode of God called *Vaikuṇṭha*. Among those who enter God's abode, some of a higher calibre attain nearness (*sāmīpya*) to God. Among those close to God, there are those who acquire the external form (*sārūpya*) of God and whose enjoyment is similar to God's. Finally, there are those souls who become united (*sāyujya*) with God, and who share his bliss. Their emancipation is of the highest type. This unity with God is by no means the identity of *ātman* and *brahman* advocated by Śaṃkara.

Even in the state of liberation, souls are distinct from God and from each other. Rāmānuja does not distinguish gradations of bliss among souls in the state of *mokṣa*.

Conclusion

While there is clearly a plurality of perspectives on human nature and destiny within Hinduism, there is also a significant sharing of outlook. There is an optimism about human nature which is reflected in defining the basic problem as one of ignorance (*avidyā*). Liberation entails a correct understanding of ourselves in relation to that which is real in the universe. For Śaṃkara, that relationship is one of identity, while for Rāmānuja it is one of inseparability. *Mokṣa* liberates us from untruth, in the most profound sense, to truth. *Mokṣa* also implies freedom from craving and desire, and the attainment of a condition of fullness and sufficiency. It is synonymous with the attainment of bliss and peace, regarded as innate to the nature of the self. The *Bhagavadgītā* (2: 70) beautifully compares the fullness of the liberated person to an ocean, the level of which is unchanged even by the waters of gushing rivers. Similarly, entering desires are absorbed in the contented mind of the liberated one.

To be human is to be part of a universal moral order in which we assume responsibility for our actions and their consequences. The doctrine of *karma*, common to all traditions of Hinduism, affirms this faith in an eternal moral order. Liberation, however, also implies freedom from *karma* and the consequent cycle of births and deaths. *Karma*, however, is only one link in a causal chain that originates with ignorance (*avidyā*) and greedful desire (*kāma*). We are liberated from *karma* and *saṃsāra* because ignorance can be overcome. All *karma*, in the words of the *Bhagavadgītā* (4: 37) is destroyed by wisdom, even as a burning fire reduces fuel to ashes. The freedom from *karma/saṃsāra* means, of course, freedom from the uncertainty of change, equated, in many scriptural passages, with the attainment of immortality and fearlessness.

For Śaṃkara, this condition of liberation is to be attained here and now. It is a freedom from a private self into one which is shared with all existence. In the *Bhagavadgītā* (6: 32) it implies a greater sensitivity towards, and awareness of, others and the ability to share their joys and sorrows:

> One, O Arjuna, who sees with equality everything, in the image of one's own self, whether in pleasure or in pain, is considered a perfect yogi.

The *Bhagavadgītā* twice (5: 25; 12: 4) uses the expression, *sarvabhūtahite ratāḥ* (delighting in the welfare of all) to describe the liberated person, showing clearly that its vision of *mokṣa* is one which draws us into relationships of unity and compassion with all beings.

NOTES

Abbreviations used
BSBS *Brahmasūtra bhaṣya of Śaṃkara*
VC *Vivekacūḍāmaṇi*
VCR *The Vedantāsūtras with the Commentary of Rāmānuja*

1. The four *varṇa*s are the priests (brahmans), secular leaders (*kṣatriya*s), merchants (*vaiśya*s), and servants (*śūdra*s). The four stages or *āśrama*s are the student (*brahmacārin*), the householder (*gṛhastha*), semi-retirement (*vānaprastha*) and renunciation (*saṅnyāsin*).
2. The *Advaita* view is that the evolution of the material universe proceeds from finer and subtle forms of matter to gross forms. See Chapter VII of Swami Madhavananda trans., *The Vedānta Paribhāṣa of Dharmarāja Adhvarīndra* (Belur Math: The Ramakrishna Mission, 1972).
3. See Swami Nikhilananda trans., *Ātmabodha of Śrī Śaṅkarācārya* (Madras: Sri Ramakrishna Math, 1975), Vs. 13.
4. See *Taittirīya Upaniṣad* II. i. 1.
5. See Ganganatha Jha trans., *The Chāndogyopaniṣad with the Commentary of Śaṅkara* (Poona: Oriental Book Agency, 1942). See VI. xvi. 3.
6. For a detailed discussion of Prabhupada's views see A.C. Bhaktivedanta Swami Prabhupada, *The Bhagavadgītā As It Is* (Los Angeles, The Bhaktivedanta Book Trust, 1981).

FURTHER READING

Chatterjee, S. (1970) *The Fundamentals of Hinduism*, Calcutta, University of Calcutta.
Chatterjee, S. and Datta, D. (1968) *An Introduction to Indian Philosophy*, Calcutta, University of Calcutta.

Gambhirananda, Swami, trans. (1965–6) *Eight Upaniṣads: with the Commentary of Śaṅkarācārya*, Calcutta, Advaita Ashrama.

Gambhirananda, Swami, trans. (1977) *The Brahma-Sūtra-Bhāṣya of Śaṅkarācārya*, Calcutta, Advaita Ashrama.

Madhavananda, Swami, trans. (1978) *Vivekacūḍāmaṇi of Śaṅkarācārya*, Calcutta, Advaita Ashrama.

Organ, T.W. (1970) *The Hindu Quest for the Perfection of Man*, Ohio, Ohio University Press.

Prasad, R.C., ed. and trans. (1991) *Śrī Rāmacaritamānasa of Tulsīdāsa*, Delhi, Motilal Banarsidass.

Radhakrishnan, S., trans. (1976) *The Bhagavadgītā*, London, Allen and Unwin.

Radhakrishnan, S., trans. (1977) *Indian Philosophy*, 2 vols, London, Allen and Unwin.

Rambachan, A. (1991) *Accomplishing the Accomplished: The Vedas as a Source of Valid Knowledge in Śaṅkara*, Honolulu, University of Hawaii Press.

Rambachan, A. (1989) 'The Value of the World as the Mystery of God in Advaita', *Journal of Dharma* 14 (July–Sept. 1989), pp. 287–97.

Sharma, A.C. (1976) *A Critical Survey of Indian Philosophy*, Delhi, Motilal Banarsidass.

Smith, H. (1958) *The Religions of Man*, New York, Harper and Row.

Thibaut, G., trans. (1990) *The Vedānta Sūtras with the Commentary of Rāmānuja*, Delhi, Motilal Banarsidass.

4. Islam

Martin Forward

According to the teaching of Islam, the destiny of human beings is life after death, either in heaven or hell. The animal, plant and mineral worlds have no existence beyond this world. Alone among God's creation, the human species has a moral sense: by their actions, people achieve their own fate.[1]

People need guidance, so that they know how to behave, and can be rewarded or punished accordingly. The Qur'ān is 'guidance for humankind' (in Arabic, *hudan li'l-nāṣ*; *sūrah* 2: 185 and many other places). This is Islam's scripture, revealed piecemeal by God through the angel Gabriel (*Jibrā'īl*) to Muhammad, the 'seal of the prophets' (33: 40), from 610 CE to shortly before his death in 632.[2] It records the exact words of the one God, who calls human beings to submit to his will: *islām* literally means 'submission'. The teachings of the Qur'ān are supplemented by the traditions (*ḥadīth*) about the Prophet Muhammad. In Islam, *ḥadīth* (tradition) has the specialist sense of being a record of the sayings and doings of Muhammad and his closest followers, as witnessed by those followers, his *ṣaḥabah* or 'companions'. There are many collections of *ḥadīth*. Muslims hold six in particular respect, and, of these, two are especially famous, those of Muhammad b. Isma'il al-Bukhari (810–870) and Abu'l Husayn Muslim b. al-Hajjaj (817–875). These two collections together are called 'The Two Ṣaḥīḥs'. *Ṣaḥīḥ* (meaning, 'sound') is a technical term in *ḥadīth* criticism, indicating the highest level of trustworthiness in a tradition. A much later and less satisfactory collection than these six is the *Mishkāt al-Māṣabīḥ*, originally put together by Imam Husayn al-Baghawi. Two centuries later, it was revised by Shaikh Wali al-Din, who gave it its present name, which means 'niche for lights'. In the South Asian subcontinent, it is widely used among Sunni Muslims (those who follow the *sunnah*, or 'manner of life' of Muhammad, recorded in the *Ḥadīth* and developed Muslim law – about ninety per cent of all Muslims). So some of the *ḥadīth* it records have been included in this chapter.

On the basis of the Qur'ān and *Ḥadīth*, scholars of jurisprudence assembled and codified the law. So certain of the teachings of eminent jurists, scholars who have interpreted Islamic law, are recorded.

The human vocation

The first human being was Adam, who was created as God's vicegerent.[3] The angels remonstrated with God, asking him why he would create a corrupter and shedder of blood. God told them that he knew something they did not. Most scholars have taken this to mean that God endowed Adam and other human beings with the capacity for moral choice and responsibility. Not even the angels have been thus endowed, and so, at God's command, they bowed down to Adam, except for Iblīs (Satan or the devil), who thereby became unfaithful. God then provided Adam with a wife, and set them in a garden, but forbade them to approach a particular tree. Satan made them stumble, and caused them to be expelled from the Garden, down to earth. Nevertheless, Adam received words of inspiration from God, and was told that anyone who follows God's guidance shall have no fear or ever grieve, whereas those who reject faith and disbelieve God's signs will forever abide in fire (2: 30–9).

There are three details which emerge from this account, relevant to the theme of this chapter: the role of human beings; the nature and limits of human disobedience; and the relationship of men and women. This story is similar to the account in the first three chapters of Genesis, the first book of the Jewish and Christian Bibles. But there are significant differences, some of which will be noted.

Adam was created as God's *khalīfah* (successor) on earth (2: 30), and Muslims believe that this responsibility has passed to his descendants, the human species. This species' link with other existent things is clear, but so is a certain distance from them: all living beings are made from water (21: 30), including human beings (25: 54), who are also said to be created from dust and from a sperm-drop (35: 11), and inbreathed by some of God's spirit (15: 29). In the Genesis account of creation, the first man named the other living creatures, and what he called them, that was their name. However, in the qur'ānic accounts, God taught Adam the names of everything. Muslims have always followed their scripture and been careful to stress the ultimate authority of God. Human beings may be his successors, but their capacity for abusing their role or seriously departing from it is severely limited: they are, after all, created from dust!

The role for humans is a moral one. The Qur'ān warns: 'We [God] did not create the heavens and the earth and all that is between them as a sport' (21: 16).[4] There is a serious purpose behind creation, particularly the creation of human beings. They are called to do good deeds, to act on behalf of God who, at the beginning of every qur'ānic *sūrah* save one, is described as *al-raḥmān al-raḥīm*, 'the merciful, the compassionate'.[5] The pursuit of goodness, truth and beauty is what gives meaning to a Muslim's life.

Human beings were created to obey God's will. What, then, is God like? Although human nature is analysed in the Qur'ān and Muslim law which developed from it, God's nature is not extensively discussed. Muslims think it impertinent and unnecessary for human beings to seek to analyse God's nature too closely. They need to know that he is one, that he has no offspring, that he calls them to obey him, and opens before them the prospect of living for ever, either in heaven or hell. They do not need to know much more about him, or why he has opened this destiny to the human species. God is described by Muslims elliptically. He is believed to have 'the most beautiful names' (*al-asmā' al-ḥusna*), most of which are found in the Qur'ān, and which describe some aspect of his activity towards humans or even a part of his nature. For example, we have seen that he is *raḥmān* and *raḥīm*. It is significant that Muslims believe there to be ninety-nine such names, one short of a round number, reminding themselves that God cannot be known in the round. He remains mysterious, beyond the power of people to grasp, physically or mentally. This reluctance to define the indefinable has remained characteristically Islamic. For example, in medieval times scholars argued that God had attributes like a hand and a face, because these were mentioned in the Qur'ān, but that these 'attributes of God' (*ṣifāt Allāh*) had to be accepted by the faithful, *bilā kayfā*, 'without knowing how'.

If God's nature eludes description, his will does not. He has provided *hudan li'l-nāṣ*, guidance for humankind, to prevent or overcome their disobedience.

Human disobedience and divine guidance

Some Christian readings of the story of humankind's first act of disobedience have created a cosmic drama of salvation: humans have fallen from grace, and the sin of Adam is overcome by the obedience of Jesus Christ. Muslims have a less dramatic view of human sin. Human beings can cleave to the good as much as to the bad. They have no innate attraction to evil: the doctrine of original sin, in any of its Christian forms, is foreign to Islam.

In Islam, human nature is not corrupt; people are not fallen and unable to save themselves, as some Christian anthropologies teach. Indeed, the Arabic word for salvation (*najāt*) is found only twice in the Qur'ān (40: 41), and it and its cognate forms have not acquired the many layers of meaning which Christians give that concept. Rather, human beings are forgetful of God, and need reminding of his will, and of the fact that he will hold them accountable for their actions on the Day of Judgement. The Qur'ān describes Adam's sin, not as a calamitous act of defiance, but as forgetfulness: 'We had already made a covenant with Adam which he forgot. We found that he had no firm resolve' (20: 115).

The concept of the 'remembrance of God' (*dhikr Allāh*) is very important: 'Believers! Do not let your wealth or your children divert you from the remembrance of God. Those who do so will be the losers' (63: 9). In the collection of *ḥadīth* by Muslim, one section is called *kitāb al-dhikr*, 'The Book of Remembrance'. The first tradition recorded in this portion is dear to many Muslims:

> Abu Huraira [a companion of the Prophet] reported God's messenger (may peace be upon him) as saying that Allah, the Exalted and Glorious, thus stated: I am near to the thought of My servant as he thinks about Me, and I am with him as he remembers Me. And if he remembers Me in his heart, I also remember him in My Heart, and if he remembers Me in assembly [of communal prayers] I remember him in assembly, better than his (remembrance), and if he draws near Me by the span of a palm, I draw near him by the cubit, and if he draws near Me by the cubit I

> draw near him by the space (covered by) two hands. And if he walks towards Me, I rush towards him.[6]

Muslims do not believe that human beings require a divinely inspired rescue package, in which God himself takes the initiative and enters human life. Rather, humankind needs divine guidance. They need God's 'signs' (*āyāt*), so that they turn from doubt to faith, and thus, after this earthly life, enter heaven and not hell. God says: 'We will show them our signs on the horizons and in their own selves, until it becomes clear to them that this is the truth' (41: 53). The whole of creation, including animals, trees, mountains, and human semen are signs which disclose the fact that all things were made by God and conform to his will. Some people spurn God's signs: 'They say: "What is there but our life in this world? We shall die and we shall live, and nothing but time can destroy us". But they have no knowledge about that; they are merely presuming' (45: 24). Such cynicism is unfounded:

> Among God's signs are night and day, the sun and moon. Do not bow before the sun and moon, but bow to God who created them, if you wish to worship him. If some [human beings] act arrogantly, others are in the presence of God and praise him night and day, never tiring of it. Among his signs, you see the ravaged earth, but when we send down rain upon it, it stirs and sprouts. The one who brings life to it is the one who brings life to the dead, for he is all-powerful. Those who distort our signs are never hidden from us. Is someone better who will be thrown on the fire, or someone who comes through safely on the Day of Resurrection? Do what you wish; God observes all you do.
>
> (41: 37–40)

It is, therefore, quite literally of eternal importance for human beings to recognise and act on the signs of God. These signs can be ignored or misread. A true reading of them points to a Day of Judgement when a person's everlasting fate beyond this world will be revealed.

The signs of creation are, to some extent, oblique. There is a more direct way of knowing God's will, through the revelation of scripture. Muhammad, the last of the prophets, brought the final, most trustworthy scripture: the Qur'ān is the 'clear sign' (15: 1), 'Mercy and a Reminder to those who believe' (29: 51). The Arabic word for qur'ānic verses is *āyāt*, 'signs' of God. Revelation is a less ambiguous sign, pointing to God, than is the natural world.

The guidance God gave Adam when he expelled him and his wife from the Garden included signs, but also words. Human beings need clarity as well as, indeed more than, subtlety. Since their ultimate destiny depends on obedience to God, they need to know what he requires, and the words of revelation provide a clearer sign than the scanning of creation's signs. Scripture provides the basis of that knowledge, as it is interpreted and worked out in Muslim law.[7]

Men and women

According to the qur'ānic accounts, the first man and woman both disobeyed God by approaching the tree he forbade them to, and so both are equally culpable (17: 19–25). Indeed, another account of the story places the major onus of disobedience on Adam (20: 120–2). Although Iblīs instigated this disobedience, and the bad deeds of all human beings since then, people cannot excuse themselves by blaming him: 'You [Iblīs] will have no authority over any of my [God's] servants, except those who put themselves in the wrong by following you' (15: 42).

In Islam, men and women are, in great measure, equal in many things, not just in their responsibility for disobedience. God accepts the good deeds of both sexes: 'I shall never waste the endeavours of any worker among you' (3: 195). Although Adam was created first, both he and his wife are equally the parents of the human species: 'O humankind! we have made you from a male and a female, so that you may know one another' (26: 13).

At the present time, and especially in the western world, the role of women in all religions is under close scrutiny. The patriarchal character of most religions is particularly questioned. This and other related issues are the concern of *Women in Religion*, also in this series. The specific task of this chapter is to ask whether there are intrinsic differences between male and female natures as created by God.

Certain aspects of the marriage relationship sharply illustrate the respective status and roles of men and women. Islamic teaching about marriage and divorce gives women important roles and rights, but places them, in certain important respects, in a subordinate role to men.

Islam teaches that marriages are not made in heaven, but here on earth. Marriage is not a sacrament but a legal contract, with three requirements. First, two adults must freely consent to marry each other. A minor may be given in marriage by his or her parents, but on reaching adulthood (an age which varies in different parts of the Muslim world), everyone has the right to reject these arrangements. Secondly, there are two dowries, both paid by the male to the female. Before marriage, he gives her gifts of jewellery and clothing which are hers and cannot be taken back without her consent. The other is a commitment undertaken in case the marriage ends in divorce, so that the woman then has the certainty of financial support. This is because a husband can divorce his wife by repudiation in front of witnesses, whereas a wife has the more difficult task of recourse to the decision of a court, where she has to establish a legal reason for termination of the marriage, such as cruelty, adultery, or lack of support. The final requirement is that two male witnesses must be present at a marriage, or, less usually, three people if only one of them is a man, and they must attest to its contents or terms: a marrying couple can add their own conditions to the three essential requirements. Women have the major responsibility for bringing up the children of a marriage. Islam makes much of the acquisition of religious knowledge, and Muslims believe that mothers have the particular responsibility of teaching their offspring the rudiments of faith. Hence the well-known and oft-quoted tradition: 'Paradise lies at the feet of the mother'. But children are usually regarded as the husband's. After a divorce, a woman is forbidden to remarry for at least three months. There are a number of reasons for this, including the necessity of determining whether she is pregnant, so that the child's paternity is known.

This brief description of the marriage relationship illustrates a certain ambiguity about the comparative status of men and women in Islam. In marriage, women are accorded an honoured role, particularly that of mother. They are also guaranteed a large measure of financial security. However, in the modern world, some Muslim women claim that the laws and customs which relate to marriage unfairly favour men, on the grounds that these arrangements and roles are fashioned for them – an example of condescension and not true partnership. Many Muslims (particularly

Muslim men) prefer to stress the fact that in pre-Islamic Arabia, the role of women was execrable: female babies were often left to die, and women of all ages had no protection, whereas Islam vastly improved the lot of women by legislating for their independent well-being. But the first part of this argument is unconvincing. Some women were important members of society: indeed, the Prophet's first wife, Khadijah, was a wealthy and independent merchant, who supported her husband financially as well as emotionally.

Controversial aspects of marriage in Islam include polygamy and *mut'ah* ('temporary') marriage, which can be interpreted as the exploitation of women by men. Polygamy, or more properly, polygyny, the marriage of one man to more than one woman, is permitted in Islam: 'If you feel you cannot deal justly towards orphans, then marry women of your choice, two, three or four. But if you cannot act justly towards them, then only one' (4:3). Some Muslim modernists have argued that since it is impossible to act justly towards more than one woman in a marriage arrangement, God's word is tantamount to a command to observe monogamy.[8] This is to invite the retort, not necessarily polemical in intent, that it is hard to see why God should legislate for an impossibility.[9] A more credible interpretation of this revelation arises from its context in the early days of Islam. The skirmishes with Makkan opponents led to the creation of orphans and widows in the nascent Muslim community, who needed the protection of marriage if they were not fortunate enough to be financially secure. Thus, polygyny was one, arguably temporary, way of providing such security. On this interpretation, it is clear that polygyny, as practised by the Prophet and his earliest male followers, was not a means of exploitation, but rather of providing widows and orphaned female young women with the stability of family life, and its economic and social support systems.

Mut'ah is a form of marriage for a fee – not a dowry – contracted for a short duration, even of just one night. This is permitted by the law of the *ithnā 'Ash'arīyah*, the majority branch of Shi'ah Islam, but is repugnant to most other Muslims, who regard it as little better than licensed prostitution. It is worth recording this custom, not because it is a widespread or integral part of Islam as a whole, which it is not, but because it poses the question of whether the emphasis upon any discussion of natural differences between men and women reveals more about men than about women. The practice of *mut'ah* marriage by a small number of Muslims and the more widespread practice of female seclusion (*purdah*, from a Persian and Urdu word, meaning 'veil' or 'curtain', a custom not commended by the Qur'ān, which enjoins only modesty [24: 30 ff.]), suggest that the real problem might be a male one – specifically, the tendency of many men to dominate those who are physically weaker than themselves, especially their wives. The Qur'ān itself seems to point to man's greater strength, which should lead him to care for rather than dominate women: 'Men should protect and support women since God has given some people more [strength?] than others' (4: 34).

Polygyny, *mut'ah* marriage, *purdah* and other practices may well be examples of male abuse of Islam, and specifically Islamic marriage, as it should be practised, but it has to be faced that God's word in the Qur'ān implies a role for women which many may now see as condescending towards them. Thus, *sūrah* 4, called 'Women', contains discussions of their familial, social and economic roles which, on the surface, strike an uncomfortable note in the modern world. One response might be: so much the worse for contemporary assumptions about human nature, given that God's word condemns it or, at least, points in other directions. Another, more helpful rejoinder, would be to examine very carefully the qur'ānic texts, the *ḥadīth*, and other examples of past Islamic practice and reflection, in an endeavour to clear away cultural and male prejudices, and to see if the religion offers different interpretations, more conducive to modern thinking.

An even more convincing way out of this impasse lies in recognising that the Qur'ān's major concern about the role and nature of men and women lies elsewhere. It does not provide a psychological or physiological blueprint of what it means to be a man or a woman. Rather, it emphasises the mutual and enriching relationship between them.

Adam's wife is not named in the Qur'ān, where she is called *zawj*, which means 'spouse' or 'partner'. Later Muslim authors called her Ḥawwā, and recorded that, after an initial separation from Adam when they were cast out of the Garden, they met again at Arafat, a plain about thirteen miles from Makkah. Arafat comes from an Arabic verb meaning 'to recognise one another'. This story of re-encounter brings into sharp focus the Muslim emphasis upon the centrality of marriage and the family: men and women are not created to be separate, but to live within the state of marriage. According to God's word, all things from the beginning of creation were made in pairs (e.g. 13: 3; 51: 49).

Thus, Christian monasticism is condemned in the Qur'ān as an invention which God has not prescribed (52: 27). Even many followers of the Ṣūfī (or, mystical) way in Islam, which orthodox Muslims often suspect as innovative and marginal to true obedience, have been married. Also, homosexuality is regarded as a major perversion, as the qur'ānic story of Lut (the biblical Lot) spells out, with Lut's words to his people: 'Of everyone in the universe, do you approach males, ignoring any wives whom God has created for you? You are, indeed, transgressors!' (26: 166 ff.). Lut and his family (except for an old woman) were spared by God, but the rest were annihilated.

The point is that human beings were created in pairs, like other creatures, for purposes of procreation, but also for mutual comfort: 'He is the one who created you [human beings] from a single soul, and made its partner from it, so he might settle down with her' (7: 189). This reference to a single soul is also a telling argument that, even if the roles of men and women differ in Muslim teaching, their origin and nature do not. Men and women, in a family, form a small community, obedient to God.

An obedient *ummah*

The concept of *ummah*, or community, is central in Islam. Muslims believe that God has put people (and, indeed, other creatures) in communities. The basic human community is the family, then widened to cover the extended family, the local, regional and larger groupings. Muhammad himself grew up as a member of the clan of *Hāshim* in the tribe of *Quraysh*. In the contemporary world, many Muslims do not live in clans and tribes, though others do. However, most Muslims are conscious of particular regional or linguistic loyalties. For example, in many places in the United Kingdom, Panjābi-speaking Muslims will go to a different mosque from Gujarati-speaking Muslims. The internal dynamics of each group (for example, how they organise themselves socially and economically) are often quite different, as are certain customs (such as eating different kinds of food, cooked in dissimilar ways). These groups are not necessarily competitive or mutually antagonistic, although, since human nature is sometimes disobedient to God's law, they may sometimes be so.

Human beings are capable of a plurality of loyalties. Hence, Muslims may be loyal to their regional language, cuisine and other customs, and good citizens of the country where they live, but their ultimate fidelity is to Islam. There are many religious communities now, as there were at the time of the Prophet. He had contact with Jews and Christians, as well as Arab pagans, but all were – for one reason or another and to a greater or lesser extent – disobedient to God's will. In particular, all these groups were guilty of polytheism: the Jews worshipped Ezra and the Christians, Jesus (9: 30); and the Arabs were devoted to a variety of localised deities.

Islam came into being as a godly community, uniquely aware of the unity of God and desirous of being obedient to him, and therefore the repository of a person's deepest commitment. In the Qur'ān, the Prophet was instructed to say: 'My prayer and service, my living and dying, belong to God, Lord of all Creation. He has no partner: with that [message] I am commanded, and I am the first Muslim' (6: 162). Elsewhere the Qur'ān says: 'God witnesses that there is no god save he, as do the angels, and people who have [revelatory] knowledge and uphold justice. There is no god but he, the almighty, the wise. The true religion with God is Islam' (3: 18 ff.).

At the very end of his life, during his farewell pilgrimage to the plain of Arafat, Muhammad received a revelation which included: 'This day I [God] have perfected your religion for you, completed my favour towards you, and have chosen for you Islam as your religion' (5: 3). Islam is a perfected religion, revealing, through its scripture, the 'clear signs' of God.

Since such a community is what God intends for all human beings, Muslims have a responsibility to encourage others to join it. Muslims have a mission to proclaim God as he really is, and to explain what he demands of humankind, and why. The Arabic word for mission is *da'wāh*, which has connotations of 'invitation' or 'call'. The Qur'ān says: 'We [God] have made you [Muslims] a moderate community so that you may be witnesses for humankind, just as the Messenger is a witness for you' (2: 143).

Muslims have interpreted 'moderate' to mean that Islam was

created to avoid the extravagances or excesses of other communities. For example, the food laws in Islam mark a middle way between the formalism of Jewish rules, and the lack of rules in Christianity.[10] We have already recorded that Islam condemns Christian monasticism, and its highly dramatic interpretation of the Fall and the salvation of humanity. The Muslim community refuses to dramatise or to underplay the human condition. It offers a middle way between extreme interpretations. Developed Muslim law prescribes a series of actions which people can follow, and thus know that they are obedient to God. It also lays down reparations for bad behaviour, so that (for example) someone who misses one of the prayer-times can make up that omission later, and find, in the laws of Islam how he or she can do so. Muslims take pride in their belief that Islam is a rational religion, aware of human nature; it imposes ways of obedience appropriate to that nature, which is neither fallen nor perfect, but prone to forgetfulness.

Because Islam spells out, more clearly than any other community, the need to obey God and, with its 'clear scripture' and framework of law, offers the means to do so, many Muslims believe that it is incumbent upon them to defend it. Hence, their concern with *jihād* ('struggle'), and *riddah* ('apostasy'). Some minority groups in Islam regard *jihād* as the sixth *arkān al-dīn* ('pillar of religion'),[11] so important is it to them that Islam should always exist, because it is the only completely committed and obedient community. Some Muslim modernists interpret *jihād* to intend an internal struggle for obedience, at least as much as an external force against others. Many base this on 9: 20: 'Those who believe and go into exile and strive (*jihād*) in the cause of God with their property and own selves, have higher rank with God. They are achievers'. Yusuf Ali comments about this verse:

> Here is a good description of *Jihād*. It *may* require fighting in God's cause, as a form of self-sacrifice. But its essence consists in (1) a true and sincere Faith, which so fixes its gaze on God, that all selfish or worldly motives seem paltry and fade away, and (2) an earnest and ceaseless activity, involving the sacrifice (if need be) of life, person or property, in the service of God. Mere brutal fighting is opposed to the whole spirit of *Jihād*, while the sincere scholar's pen or preacher's voice or wealthy man's contributions may be the most valuable forms of *Jihād*.[12]

Apostasy is particularly reprehensible, for a number of reasons. One is, if you have been shown God's clear signs, yet reject them, that is manifest and perverse error. Another is psychological: the effect of a member who leaves, upon a community which strives in the way of God to do his will, particularly when it is a minority community. The Qur'ān prescribes punishment for a *murtadd* ('one who turns back', apostate), not on earth but only in the life to come, which will be a 'dreadful penalty' (16: 106). However, many *ḥadīth* introduce the death penalty in this life for renegades. For example, according to a *ḥadīth* associated with 'A'isha, a wife of the Prophet, Muhammad permitted the killing of anyone 'who abandons religion and separates himself from the community'.

Riddah is an (or perhaps even, the) outstanding example of the tension in Islam between individual responsibility and choice on the one hand, and communal identity on the other. By and large, although individual Muslims differ in their commitment to the laws of Islam, so that (for example) some will pray the required five daily prayers, while others will pray occasionally and some not at all, few contemplate publicly withdrawing from it. Among other reasons, it is because of a conviction, or at least a sentiment, that the *ummah* of Islam is the best hope of humankind in describing how to live responsibly in this life so as to be rewarded in the next: it is the repository of the clearest and most convincing assessment of human nature and destiny.

Although human beings live in communities, which ought to, and in large parts of the (particularly non-western) world do, nurture and focus their religious loyalties, each person is responsible for his or her own deeds. Popular Islam believes in the intercession of prophets and holy men,[13] especially the intercession of Muhammad, but the weight of qur'ānic evidence points against it.

> Keep away from those who take their religion as a sport and entertainment. They are enticed by this world. Proclaim this, in case a soul should be destroyed because of what it has earned: it has no protector, no intercessor apart from God. If it offered any equivalent, none would be accepted. Those who deliver themselves to destruction for what they have done must drink boiling water and suffer agonising torment [in hell] because they were unbelievers.
>
> (6: 70)

Free will and predestination

In reality, can a person be responsible for his or her own life of faith? Many religions have struggled with this question. Islam's dilemma is more acute than most, because the word *islām* itself has connotations of 'submission', 'surrender' and 'peace'. A Muslim is a submitter to God; in submitting, he or she finds an eternal peace. Developed Muslim theology believed that God's most important attribute is his will. A religion which so clearly requires its adherents to submit to the will of the one God must necessarily be committed to his sovereign action and power. He is *al-rabb* 'the Lord', and human beings are *'abd*, 'servant'. In fact, one form of *'abd* means humankind, *al-'ibād*.

Some *ḥadīth* include as a sixth article of Muslim faith, 'the divine decree for better or worse, for sweet or bitter'.[14] This belief arises from the fact that scripture seems to point in two directions: 'God has created you [human beings] and all your works' (37: 96), looks a different kind of statement from, 'On that day, every soul will be recompensed with what it has earned' (40: 17). The Qur'ān has more of the first kind of statement than the second. A particularly hard statement is: 'God opens anyone's breast to Islam whom he wants to guide, while he constricts the breast of anyone whom he wants to be led astray' (6: 125). Another uncompromising statement of God's sovereignty is: 'All things have been created after a fixed decree' (65: 3). The word translated 'decree' is, in Arabic, *qadar*. In early Islam, there was a school of theology, the Qadariyya. They were given their name because they, the champions of free will, talked about *qadar*, its opposite!

The issue of free will was fully and controversially discussed in medieval times, and it divided Muslims more than any other question. In so far as any solution was reached, it was the doctrine of *kasb*, 'acquisition', by which God creates an action, but an individual acquires it. So, for example, a murderer and a benefactor are responsible for different kinds of achievements, by virtue of acquiring the deeds which God has created for them. This is a bold attempt to solve an intractable problem, but it is not especially convincing, even to many Muslims. Basically, the doctrine of *kasb* upholds *qadar*. Certainly, common parlance among Muslims points more to a belief in determination than in free will. Most Muslims always add to a state of intention, the suffix, *in Shā'a Allāh*, 'if God wills': 'We shall go tomorrow, if God wills'. Among other expressions often used by Muslims are: 'it is written', 'it is decided' and 'it is fate'.

There are commonsense responses to the issue of determination or free will which point in a less fatalistic direction. Because the Qur'ān describes one God, whom alone people ought to worship, and tells of the destiny of those who obey and those who disobey him, it would be extraordinary if human beings had no control over their actions. In practice, most Muslims act as if they were responsible people, with choices to make. Muslim scholars are reluctant to grant too much freedom of choice to human beings, lest it undermine their belief in God's sovereign will. There is much to be said for their scepticism. Although many people in the West value freedom of choice, in practice it is, for most people, severely limited. Everybody is constrained by accident of genes to 'acquisitions' of colour, intelligence, and, perhaps, even such things as musicality and health. Moreover, many people are imprisoned by poverty, so that they cannot exercise some of their 'acquisitions'. Life is much more circumscribed than recent western philosophy and consumerism have admitted. Yet, within the restrictions which govern everyone's existence, human beings can construct a life of goodness and obedience, or else evil and disobedience. This is what much of Islamic theology has taught or assumed.

The Last Day

One of the articles of faith is *qiyāmat*, or 'resurrection'. The first *sūrah*, called *fātiḥah* or 'opening', which Muslims recite many times each day, calls to mind God as 'Master of the Day of Judgement' (1: 4). At the very beginning of his ministry, Muhammad was told to 'stand up and warn!' (74: 2). The warning was about the certainty of a Day of Judgement that will overtake everyone.

Eight particular features characterise the Muslim view of the last things: the signs, the sounding of the trumpets, the appearance of God, the descent of the records, the scales, the bridge, the Prophet's basin, and his intercession.

There are several signs of the Last Day. Some of these are given in detail in the *Ḥadīth*, but not the Qur'ān. They include the darkening of sun and moon, tumult and war, and the decline of faith on earth.

The most important signs are the appearance of *al-Dajjāl*, a word which derives from Syriac and means 'the charlatan', and then of *'Īsā* (Jesus). Basically, Muslims believe that *al-Dajjāl* (who is not named in the Qur'ān) will arrive on earth during its closing days. He will oversee forty years (or forty days) of injustice and license, after which Jesus will destroy him. After he has slaughtered *al-Dajjāl*, Jesus will restore faith, and the whole world will convert to Islam. Muhammad is reported to have said:

> By Him in whose hand my soul is, the son of Mary will soon descend among you as a just judge. He will break crosses, kill swine and abolish the *jizyah* [a poll-tax on non-Muslim monotheists in areas ruled by Muslims] and wealth will pour forth to such an extent that no one will accept it, and one *sajdah* [prostration] will be better than the world and what it contains.
>
> (Reported by Abu Huraira, in Robson 1970: 1159)

Jesus will live for forty years, die and be buried at Madinah, beside Muhammad, in a vacant space between Abu Bakr and 'Umar, Muhammad's immediate successors as political head (*khalīfah*) of the Muslim community.

On the Last Day, there will be 'a blast on the trumpet, when all in the heavens and on earth will lose consciousness (or die), except those whom God has exempted. Then there will be another blast and suddenly they will arise and look around' (39: 68). Certain *ḥadīth* name the trumpet blower as the angel *Isrāfīl*, and give great detail about him. For example, the spirits of some of the dead who await the Day of Resurrection live in the holes of his mighty trumpet.

Then God will appear as the only eternal being: 'everything will perish but his face' (28: 88). He will be revealed as the only abiding entity, majestic and glorious, just as he was before he created anyone or anything. His justice will be blazed abroad at a large court of justice where all people must appear to hear God's verdict on them.

After the trumpet blasts and God's appearance, people will wait for forty years before they are judged. Some will wander around; others will stand and look upwards, awaiting the books; all will perspire because of their great sorrow. During this time, the recording angels will give up to God the books in which they have written of people's good and bad deeds. Each book will be given by the angels to its owner. The just will hold it in their right hand, the wicked behind their backs (84: 7–12) or in their left hand (69: 25). It will be said to each person: 'Read your book!; today, there is nobody but yourself who calls you to account' (17: 14).

Then each person's deeds will be weighed on scales (42: 17). It is believed that the angels Gabriel and Michael (*Mikā'īl*) will watch over this event. Some scholars say that good deeds will appear bright, and bad ones gloomy. According to the Qur'ān:

> Once the trumpet is blown, no ties of kinship will exist between them [people] on that day, nor will they be able to question one another. Those whose scales are heavy will prosper, while those whose scales are light will lose their souls – they will abide in hell. The fire will scorch their faces as they burn away in it.
>
> (23: 101–4)

Moreover, one group of sinners (those who slander chaste women, though some *ḥadīth* widen this group to include all who are wicked) will be tormented severely 'on that day when their tongues, hands and feet will testify against them about what they have been doing' (24: 24).

After this, everyone must pass the *ṣirāṭ al-jahīm* ('bridge of hell'). The Qur'ān records that evildoers, their spouses, and any object of their worship other than the one God, must walk this way (37: 22 ff.), but later *ḥadīth* indicate that all must attempt to cross. Some Muslims will get to the other side, whereas others will fall into hell, from which they will later be rescued. Unbelievers will fall headlong into hell, and remain there for ever. There is abundant post-qur'ānic material about this bridge: for example, it is very thin and sharp, and has seven arches.

One further event, not mentioned in the Qur'ān, but commonplace in Muslim accounts of the Last Day, is the Prophet's basin (*ḥawḍ*). It is the pool in Paradise, usually located at the other side of the *ṣirāṭ al-jahīm*, where Muhammad will meet members of the Islamic community. It is filled with delicious liquid, a foretaste of paradisal joys. Some *ḥadīth* describe it as a place of purification from sin, before entry to Paradise, after the Prophet's intercession (*shafā'ah*) with God for sinners.

The popular belief that Muhammad intercedes on the Day of

Judgement, to mitigate, shorten or remit the sojourn in hell of believers who have sinned, is frowned on by many Muslim theologians, but is nevertheless held by most Muslims. Most qur'ānic verses forbid anyone's intercession, even Muhammad's: 'Heed the day when no soul will be able to pay indemnity for another. No intercession will be accepted from him, nor will any alternative be accepted from it. They will not be helped' (2: 48). Yet the celebrated 'throne-verse' includes the statement: 'Who can intercede with him except by his permission?' (2: 255). This sounds as though there may be some scope for intercession, which most Muslims believe. Some of the *Mu'tazila*, a group of medieval theologians whose views (which were disparate and remain difficult to pin down exactly) were eventually condemned by Sunni Muslims, argued that the intercession of Muhammad was for the increase of merit, not to thwart punishment. A more influential view has been that Muhammad intercedes for those Muslims who have committed great sins.

The final abode of human beings

Muslims depict three locations for people after the Last Day: limbo, heaven and hell. A veil lies between heaven and hell, disclosing an intermediate state:

> Between them both [the inhabitants of the Garden and the inhabitants of the Fire] a veil will hang, and on the heights will be men who know everyone by their marks. They will call out to those who inhabit the Garden, 'Peace be on you'. They have not themselves entered therein, eager though they are to do so. When their eyes are turned towards those who inhabit the Fire, they will say, 'Our Lord! Do not place us with such wrongdoers.'
>
> (7: 46 ff.)

Scholars differ greatly about the purpose of this location. Some say that it is a place of honour for prophets and saints, and the Arabic word *al-a'rāf*, which means 'elevated place' supports this interpretation. The majority, however, regard it as a site for people whose good and bad deeds, when weighed in the balance, are found to be exactly equal.

In the Qur'ān, hell is described in very physical terms. The commonest of all names for hell is *al-nar*, which means 'the Fire'. It is a terrifying place, described in the Qur'ān many times and in many ways:

> Has the story of the overshadowing ever reached you? On that day, some faces will be sunk in dismay, labouring, toiling. They will roast in a fire which scorches. They will be offered a drink from a boiling hot spring. They will have no food but a bitter, thorny plant, which will neither nourish them nor satisfy their hunger.
>
> (88: 1–7)

But who will go there, and for how long? All those whose bad deeds are more than their good ones will go there. All *mushrikūn* (those guilty of *shirk*, polytheism, or 'those who associate [other things with God]') will abide in hell forever. The Qur'ān says: 'the People of the Book who disbelieve as well as the associaters will remain in the Fire of hell; these are the worst of creatures' (98: 6).

According to most scholars, unrepentant Muslims, even those who have committed great sins, will not remain in hell forever, because of a qur'ānic verse which says: 'whoever has done an atom's weight of good will see it' (99: 8). This view is held by the Ash'arites, who follow the teaching of Abu'l-Hasan 'Ali b. Isma'il al-Ash'ari (873/4–935/6 CE), the theologian who did much to define and defend Sunni beliefs against *Mu'tazila* doctrines which he abandoned in 912/3. They believe that the Prophet will intercede for the unrepentant Muslim sinner.

The most common name by which heaven is called in the Qur'ān is *al-Jannah*, 'the Garden'. Later scholars identified various gardens of Paradise. Some located seven, which fits nicely with the seven ranks of hell that are also distinguished. Others pictured four, because in the Qur'ān it is said that there are two gardens (55: 46), and beside them two more (55: 62). Paradise (*firdaws*, a Persian word) is described in many *sūrahs*, for example:

> Immortal youths will stroll around them with glasses, pitchers, and a cup from a fountain which will not dull or intoxicate them, and fruit of their choice, and with meat from any poultry they desire. There will be damsels with sparkling eyes, like treasured pearls, a reward for their past

deeds. They will hear no frivolous or backbiting conversation, but only people saying, 'Peace, peace'.

(56: 17–26)

Throughout the history of Islam up to the present day, popular treatises contain vivid descriptions of *al-Jannah*, detailing its sensuous pleasures. They build on the basic qur'ānic description of it as a garden filled with beautiful women and youths, couches covered in rich brocades, wonderful drink and food. Certain *ḥadīth* also describe its physical delights:

> Anas reported the Prophet as saying, 'In paradise the believer will be given such and such power to conduct sexual intercourse.' He was asked whether he would be capable of that and replied that he would be given the capacity of a hundred men. Tirmidhi transmitted it.
>
> (Robson 1970, vol. 2: 1200)

The possibility of attaining a vision of God has been controversial. The *ḥadīth* are more or less unanimous in believing that it will happen – a terrifying experience for those hell-bound, and the supreme joy of those in heaven. al-Ash'ari taught that a vision of God was a reality for those in heaven but that its modality was beyond human comprehension, denying the *Mu'tazila* position that God would not be visible in a literal sense to people.

Some Muslims have argued that all language about the last things is metaphorical, rather than literal. In particular, exponents of *falsafah* ('philosophy') have done so, but many orthodox Muslims have regarded them as heterodox or heretical. Theologians have tended to stress the intellectual joys of heaven, but have not denied the literal truth of its delights, though they have sometimes applied the formula, *bilā kayfā*: they are true, 'without [asking] how'.

Muslim modernists have also stressed the non-literal nature of the language, but some have explained why it is so sensuous. The Indian judge and modernist writer, Syed Ameer Ali (1849–1928) argued:

> Mohammed was addressing himself not only to the advanced minds of a few idealistic thinkers who happened to be then living, but to the wide world around him engrossed in materialism of every type. He had to adapt himself to the comprehensions of all. To the wild famished Arab, what more grateful, or what more consonant to his ideas of paradise

> than rivers of unsullied incorruptible water, or of milk and honey; or anything more acceptable than unlimited fruit, luxuriant vegetation, inexhaustible fertility? He could conceive of no bliss unaccompanied by these sensuous pleasures.[15]

Many Muslim modernists, including Ameer Ali,[16] have quoted a tradition recorded in many collections, including those of Bukhari and Muslim, and interpreted it to mean that the delights of paradise are beyond the power of human words to describe literally:

> Abu Huraira told that after God's messenger had stated that God most high has said, 'I have prepared for my upright servants what eye has not seen, nor ear heard, nor has entered into the heart of man,' he added, 'Recite if you wish, "No soul knows what comfort has been concealed for them [32: 17]".'
>
> (Robson 1970, vol. 2: 1196)

Nevertheless, the majority of Muslims have believed that the language of the Qur'ān and *Ḥadīth* about the life to come is literally true. As Ameer Ali wrote: 'by far perhaps the larger class, however, believe in a literal fulfilment of all the word-paintings of the Koran'.[17]

There are important issues at stake here. One is the relationship between myth and history in Islam.[18] Another is to do with what sort of god, God is. A literal interpretation of the material in the Qur'ān and *Ḥadīth* about the Last Day portrays a harsh deity, which seems at odds with the depiction of him at the beginning of every *sūrah* save one as *al-raḥmān al-raḥīm*, 'the merciful, the compassionate'.

Certainly, few Muslims have argued that all people will enter heaven: any doctrine of universalism is alien to Islam. A broad consensus exists that, at the Last Day, the destiny of a person turns on his or her deeds – Paradise is open to those who have obeyed God's law, and hell to those who have spurned it. There is also a strong but by no means unanimous opinion that no Muslim will enter hell forever, but this may reflect the opinion of those who have seen membership of the Islamic *ummah* as an end in itself rather than the means to the end that, within it, humans should be nurtured into obedience to God.

What, however, of the final destiny of those who are not Muslims, but who have obeyed the law of God in so far as it was revealed to them? In contemporary multi-faith societies, this is not merely an academic question.

Post-qur'ānic Muslim scholarship created seven ranks of hell, based on qur'ānic passages. *Jahannam*, which is used seventy-seven times in the Qur'ān to mean 'hell', is the place for unrepentant wicked Muslims until they go to Paradise. *Laẓā* (a word found only once in the Qur'ān) is a blazing fire for Christians, and *al-ḥuṭamah* (found twice in the Qur'ān) a kindled fire for Jews. *Sa'īr* (used sixteen times in the Qur'ān for 'hell') is a blazing inferno for Sabaeans (a religious group, mentioned in the Qur'ān, whose identification is not known), and *saqar* (mentioned four times in the Qur'ān) is a scorching fire for the Zoroastrians. *al-Jahim* (used twenty-five times in the Qur'ān) is the region of hell for idolaters, and *al-hawiya*, the 'abyss' (found once in the Qur'ān), is a bottomless pit for hypocrites, those who pretend to have faith.

The Qur'ān gives no credence to these ranks, who will inhabit them, and what their fate will be like. It does, however, state: 'If anyone desires a religion other than Islam, it will never be accepted from him, and in the life to come he will be among the losers' (3: 85). Some modernists quote, against this, 'There must be no compulsion in religion' (2: 256), but the two verses are not addressing the same issue: to say that people should not be forced to believe something is not necessarily to agree that what they are permitted to believe is right or that ultimately God will accept it from them.

A more convincing alternative is provided by a qur'ānic passage which condemns Jews and Christians for judging the fate of others by their communal identity, rather than by their good deeds:

> They say, 'No one will enter the Garden unless he is a Jew or Christian'. These are their desires. Say, 'Bring forth your proof if you speak truly'. Rather, whoever submits his will to God, and does good, will receive a reward from his Lord. No fear will rest on them, and they shall not be sorrowful.
>
> (2: 111 ff.)

Because Islam is the last and final religion, and Muhammad the 'seal of the prophets' (33: 40), Muslims find it difficult to integrate post-Islamic religions like Sikhism, and heterodox Islamic movements like the Ahmadiyya[19] and the Baha'is,[20] into any scheme which values other religions. In practice, Muslims have always been able to find a role for *ahl al-kitāb*, 'People of the Book', those who have a scripture which reveals God as one, especially Jews, Christians and Zoroastrians. Some modernists have included Hinduism, Buddhism and other non-monotheistic theological and philosophical traditions as, to some extent, revealed by God.[21]

A *ḥadīth* records that the Prophet encouraged Muslims to hope that the *ummah* of Islam would constitute half of the inhabitants of Paradise:[22] this demands that other occupants of Paradise will be from other communities. The emphasis in the Qur'ān and early Islam is upon the community as a means to the end of promoting good works, not the end itself.

NOTES

1. *Sūrah* 72 recounts how the *jinn* heard the message of the Qur'ān, and, as a result, turned to the worship of the one God. Qur'ānic commentators and translators differ as to whether the *jinn* are supernatural beings, or a particular group of people. The evidence points to the former, as the vast majority of scholars agree. Nevertheless, it seems that only human beings in this material world can freely respond to God's commands, since the *jinn* are usually regarded as immaterial beings, though made of fire.
2. Muslims hold all prophets but particularly Muhammad in the greatest respect. After his name, they usually write PBUH ('Peace be upon him'). Muslims date their lunar calendar from Muhammad's *hijrah* ('emigration') to Madinah from Makkah. That event is dated 622 in the solar calendar used in the West, which has gained widespread usage as the 'Common Era', or 'Christian Era'.
3. In a number of places where the Qur'ān states that man was created from dust, Adam's name is not mentioned (e.g. 30: 20; 22: 5); nor is anyone else's. The vast majority of Muslims believe that Adam was the first man and the first prophet.
4. Muslims believe that, because their scripture was revealed in a particular language, Arabic, it can never be translated. Nevertheless, there are many English paraphrases of the Qur'ān available. Some renderings are better than others. The best is probably that of M.M. Khatib (1986) *The Bounteous Koran*, London, Macmillan. None is very satisfactory. I have offered my own interpretations in this chapter.
5. The exception is *sūrah* 9. There is no satisfactory reason for this

omission. The best suggestion is that since God's mercy and compassion form the theme of the beginning of this *sūrah*, the prefix (which Muslims regards as part of divine revelation) is here redundant.

6. A.H. Siddiqi (ed.) (1977) *Sahih Muslim by Imam Muslim*, Delhi, Kitab Bhavan, vol. 4, p. 1408.
7. For a larger discussion of the process of the coming into being of Muslim law, see the chapter on Islam in *Sacred Writings*, in this series.
8. S.A. Ali (1922 edn) *The Spirit of Islam*, London, Chatto and Windus, p. 229.
9. A. Guillaume (1954) *Islam*, London, Penguin, pp. 156 ff. Guillaume is sometimes unnecessarily and unhelpfully polemical and christianising in his comments and interpretations, but his basic point is a fair one.
10. The matter of food laws is discussed in the chapter on Islam in the book of this series entitled *Attitudes to Nature*.
11. The five pillars of Islam are, in alphabetical order: *hajj* (pilgrimage to Makkah); *ṣalāt* (ritual prayer); *ṣawm* (fasting during the month of Ramadan); *shahādah* (the profession of faith that 'There is no god but God, and Muhammad is the Prophet of God'); and *zakāt* (almsgiving).
12. A. Yusuf Ali (1988 reprint), *The Holy Qur'ān: Text, Translation and Commentary*, Lahore, Muhammad Ashraf, note 1270.
13. Popular Islam is described in the chapter on Islam in *Worship*, also in this series. The common Muslim belief in the intercession of the Prophet on the Day of Judgement is mentioned in this chapter in the sections on The Last Day and The final abode of human beings.
14. The other five articles are mentioned in 4: 136: 'whoever denies God, his angels, his scriptures, his messengers and the Last Day has wandered far astray'.
15. S.A. Ali, (1922 edn) *The Spirit of Islam*, London, Chatto and Windus, pp. 198 ff.
16. S.A. Ali, (1922 edn) *The Spirit of Islam*, London, Chatto and Windus, p. 199.
17. S.A. Ali, (1922 edn) *The Spirit of Islam*, London, Chatto and Windus, p. 200.
18. See the chapter on Islam in the book in this series entitled *Myth and History*.
19. A movement founded in 1889 by Mirza Ghulam Ahmad (1835–1908), who made a number of important claims about himself: he was an *avatāra* of the Hindu god Kṛṣṇa, the *mahdī* ('the rightly-guided one'), and the Messiah. They have split into two groups: the Qadiyanis, who believe that Ghulam Ahmad was a *nabī* ('prophet'), are clearly heretical; the Lahoris, who believe him to have been a *mujaddid*, 'renewer', are less clearly so.
20. This has become a separate religion, but it arose out of Iranian Islam.

The founder, Baha'ullah (1817–92) is regarded by Baha'is as a prophet, as is his teacher, Mirza Ali Muhammad (1819–50), the *bāb*, or 'door'.

21. S.A. Ali (1922 edn) *The Spirit of Islam*, London, Chatto and Windus, p. 111. He includes Jesus, Moses, Zoroaster, Sakya-Muni (the Buddha), and Plato among those whose work was completed by Muhammad.
22. A.H. Siddiqi (1977) *Sahih Muslim by Imam Muslim*, Delhi, Kitab Bhavan, vol. 1, pp. 142–4.

FURTHER READING

Izutsu, T. (1964) *God and Man in the Koran: Semantics of the Koranic Weltanschauung*, Tokyo, Keio Institute of Cultural and Linguistic Studies.

Mernissi, F. (1991) *Women and Islam: An Historical and Theological Enquiry*, Oxford, Basil Blackwell.

Robson, J. (1970) *Mishkāt al-Māṣabiḥ, vols 1 and 2*, Lahore, Muhammad Ashraf.

Smith, J.I. and Haddad, Y.Y. (1981) *The Islamic Understanding of Death and Resurrection*, Albany, State University of New York Press.

5. Judaism

Sybil Sheridan

Rabbi Simeon said, 'When the Holy One, blessed be He, came to create Adam, the ministering angels formed themselves into groups and parties, some of them saying, 'Let him be created' whilst others urged, 'Let him not be created . . .'.

(*Bereshit* (Genesis) *Rabbah* 5: 6)

This famous *midrash*[1] sets out a basic dilemma that runs through much of Jewish thought.

Love said, 'Let him be created because he will dispense acts of love'; Truth said, 'Let him not be created, because he is compounded of falsehood'; Righteousness said, 'Let him be created because he will perform righteous deeds'; Peace said, 'Let him not be created because he is full of strife'.

Since there was no clear majority in favour or against the creation of humanity, God took Truth and threw it to earth: thus explaining the verse in Psalm 85: 'Truth springeth out of the earth; and righteousness hath looked down from heaven.'

Another version has it:

While the ministering angels were arguing with each other and disputing with each other, the Holy One, blessed be He, created him. Said He to them: 'What can ye avail? Man has already been made!'

This theme runs through much of rabbinic literature. Humanity is host to a bundle of contradictions and it is unclear whether we should celebrate or commiserate this event of creation. However, since Judaism does not demand strict conformity in thought, there is by no means only one interpretation available. Nevertheless, the underlying theme tends to be optimistic. Despite people's evil ways, they remain ever with the possibility of reconciliation with God. All God's creation is seen as 'good' (Gen. 1), but on the sixth day, after the creation of man, 'God saw everything that He had made, and behold, it was very good' (Gen. 1: 31).

The biblical accounts of the creation of humankind

And God said, 'let us make
man in our own image, after our
likeness; and let them have
dominion over the fish of the
sea and over the fowl of the air,
and over the cattle, and over all
the earth and over every
creeping thing upon the earth.'
And God created man in His
own image, in the image of God
created He him; male and
female created He them.
(Gen. 1: 26–7)

Then the Lord God formed
man out of the dust of the
ground, and breathed into
his nostrils the breath of
life; and man became a
living soul . . .

And the Lord God
took the man and put him
into the garden of Eden
to dress it and keep it.

(Gen. 2: 7, 15)

Jewish tradition sees the two accounts of creation as one continuous narrative. Rather than contradicting each other, they offer different insights into the nature of God's creation.

In the second chapter of Genesis, God fashions a person out of the earth. The Hebrew is *adam* – a generic word denoting all humanity, while the Hebrew for earth is *adamah*. *Adam* is an 'earthling' taken from the earth. The connection also shows humanity's purpose in God's world; *adam* is to tend the earth – to look after God's garden: 'to dress it and keep it'.

In the first chapter, all creatures that live on the land are formed out of the earth in a similar fashion.

> And God said; 'Let the earth bring forth the living creature after its kind, cattle and creeping thing and beast of the earth after its kind.' And it was so.
>
> (Gen. 1: 24)

Moreover, human beings and animals were created on the same day. This was understood in the *midrash* to mean that people resemble animals, not only physically, but, 'He eats and drinks like animals, procreates like animals and dies like animals' (*Bereshit Rabbah* 14: 3). The origins of humanity are, therefore, totally creaturely.

However, this is only half the story. Genesis 2: 7 continues to describe how God breathed the breath of life into the nostrils of the creature 'and he became a living being'. Two closely related Hebrew terms in this sentence offered the rabbis of the *midrash* a clue to the uniqueness of man, *nefesh* translated into the English here as 'being' and *neshamah* rendered as 'breath'. Both terms are used to mean soul, but while *nefesh* is a term used also of animals (Gen. 1: 24), *neshamah* is not. *Nefesh* is the anima found in all creatures. *Neshamah* is what is described in Genesis (1: 26–7) as the image of God in humanity.

Image of God in humanity

God's announcement that he will make humankind in his own image has resulted in a variety of interpretations. However, they all share one overriding principle: they are at pains to avoid any implied anthropomorphism – or, rather, 'deomorphism' – in the verse. Whatever can be made of the statement, it is not to mean that humans resemble God physically. The medieval rabbis had great difficult with the anthropomorphic language of the early chapters of the Bible and this is reflected in the quotations that follow.

According to *Bereshit Rabbah* 14: 3, the image of God makes '*adam*' like the angels.

> He stands upright, like the ministering angels, he speaks, he understands, he sees like the ministering angels.

Other rabbinic interpretations offer a range of suggestions. According to one such (*Sifre* to Deuteronomy 1: 13), animals are imbued with a natural or instinctive intelligence which enables them to function according to their needs and nature, but without forethought. This is known as *hokhmah* – wisdom. Human beings also possess *hokhmah*, but in addition have *binah* – understanding, the ability to make connections, the faculty of reason. Upon *binah* the whole creativity and productivity of humankind depends.

Another interpretation is that humanity mirrors on earth the activity of God in the universe. In his commentary on the verse, 'Let us make man in our own image', Shabatai Donnolo, a tenth-century physician and philosopher, wrote:

> This image and likeness of which the Blessed One spoke is not the form of the appearance of the Countenance, but the form of the work of God and His activity in the universe. As God is supreme and rules over man and over all the world, beneath and above, so is man; as God knows and discerns things that happened and foresees things to come, so man, whom God has granted wisdom to know; as God supplies and gives food to all flesh, so does man sustain all the members of his household, his attendants, and his animals; and as the Creator built the world and laid the foundations of the earth, stretched the heavens and gathered the waters together, so man is able to build, to found, and to call and gather together, to sow, to make grow, to plant and to do . . . and in most things man is likened in small measure to God, in accordance with the limitations of the strength and the short span of the life which God has given him.[2]

The contemporary philosopher, Isidore Epstein (1954), makes a further distinction between 'image' and 'likeness'. On the basis of medieval rabbinic commentary, he suggests that the image of God delineates the objective elements of God's nature – the attributes that define the divine essence, such as unity, eternity, omnipresence, omnipotence, omniscience and incorporeality. The likeness of God, on the other hand, delineates the subjective aspects of God's character, as it impresses itself on his creatures through his activity in the universe. These attributes are commonly associated with the list of thirteen described in Exodus 34: 6–7:

> The Lord, the Lord, God, merciful and gracious, longsuffering, and abundant in goodness and truth; keeping mercy unto the thousandth generation, forgiving iniquity and transgression and sin, and that will by no means clear the guilty; visiting upon the children and upon the children's children, unto the third and unto the fourth generation.

With regard to 'image', the human *neshamah* can be seen as replicating some, but not all, of the objective attributes of God's essence. The human soul is a unity, incorporeal, omnipresent and eternal; but it is not omniscient or omnipotent. It is through the *neshamah* that humans come to an understanding of what God is. In the words of Saadia Gaon:[3]

> Though his body is small, his soul is longer than heaven and earth, for through it, he reaches even what is above them and the cause of them – the creator itself.

Regarding 'likeness', the human character can emulate most, but not all, of the subjective attributes of God. Humankind has the capacity to be merciful, gracious, longsuffering and abundant in truth. But the punishment of the guilty is a task reserved for God alone.

With the capacity to emulate the subjective attributes of God comes the notion of '*imitatio Dei*' – that a person not only can, but should, imitate God and act as God in the world. The biblical basis for this is Leviticus 19: 1.

> And the Lord spoke unto Moses, saying:
> Speak unto all the congregation of the children of Israel, and say unto them:
> Ye shall be holy; for I the Lord your God am holy.

There are many expressions of this concept in rabbinic Judaism, for example, in the *midrash Tanhuma* (*Toledot* 12):

> 'After the Lord you shall walk' (Deut. 13: 5). How can man walk after God? Is He not a consuming fire? What is meant is that man ought to walk after the attributes of God. Just as the Lord clothes the naked, so you shall clothe the naked. Just as He visits the sick, so you shall visit the sick. Just as the Lord comforted the bereaved, so you shall comfort the bereaved; just as He buried the dead, so you shall bury the dead.

The creation of woman

The discrepancies in the two accounts regarding the creation of woman have given rise to a great deal of literature regarding the nature of both sexes, their relationship and their purpose.

In the first chapter of Genesis, male and female are created equally. 'In the image of God created He him; male and female created He them' (Gen. 1: 27). The nature and purpose of Man and Woman is, therefore, identical. In the second chapter:

> . . . the Lord God said: 'It is not good that the man should be alone; I will make him a help meet for him.' . . . The Lord God caused a deep sleep to fall upon the man and he slept; and He took one of his ribs, and closed up the place with flesh instead thereof. And the rib, which the Lord God had taken from the man, made He a woman, and brought her unto the man.
>
> (Gen. 2: 18, 21–22)

Here, the creation of woman is clearly different from that of man. Moreover, the purpose for woman's creation is distinctive. Woman was created because man could not find a suitable companion among the animals. The subsequent verses show clearly that her role is to be man's sexual partner.

Midrash, in elaborating on this account of creation, shows something of the prevailing view of women held in the period.

> He considered well from what part to create her. Said He; 'I will not create her from his head, lest she be swell headed; nor from the eye, lest she be a coquette; nor from the ear lest she be an eavesdropper; nor from the mouth lest she be a gossip; nor from the heart, lest she be prone to jealousy; nor from the hand, lest she be light-fingered; nor from the foot lest she be a gadabout; but from the modest part of man, for even when he stands naked, that part is covered (i.e. with flesh)'.
>
> (*Bereshit Rabbah* 18: 3)

Other rabbis were more concerned with reconciling the two accounts, however. The first account was seen by many as the prototype for all humanity. *Adam* is the generic word for all mankind, and it is only after the woman is created – *ishah* – that the male of the species is specified and called *ish*. To some, the first person was the perfect image of God – a heavenly model upon which the earthly one was based. The mystical tradition made much of *Adam kadmon* – primordial *adam* – as a purely spiritual entity that contains the divine emanations of God. Others saw the first person as human, but containing both male and female; either a hermaphrodite that later became two people, or a double-faced being who was then split into two.[4]

A later *midrash*[5] quotes a tradition that the first man had two wives. The original, Lillith, was created equally with him and refused to be dominated sexually by him. He therefore divorced her and God made Eve out of the man's rib, so that her natural longing would be to be part of him. Though from a minor and most probably heretical source, this idea has received much prominence in recent years through the women's movement, for whom Lillith has become a significant symbol.

The biblical text itself says less about the subordination of woman than it does about the purpose of her creation as partner to man and, even more importantly, about her role in bearing children. The matriarchs stand as the supreme and ideal examples of womanhood, while in rabbinic literature, the childless prophets Deborah and Hulda are sharply criticised.[6]

One popular rabbinic tradition sees God, man and woman as equal partners in the creation of children. 'There are three partners in man; the Holy One, blessed be He, his father and his mother' (B. Talmud *Niddah* 31a). The father and mother provide all the physical attributes for the child, while God,

> The Holy One, blessed be He, gives him the spirit and the soul, beauty of features, eyesight, the power of hearing and the ability to walk, understanding and discernment.

There are numerous tales of rabbis attempting to create people. Such creatures, known as *golems*, were apparently moderately successful. They could move about, obey orders, but could not speak, or think independently. Without woman, and without God's breath of life, a real human being cannot be formed.

The purpose of humanity's creation

> And God blessed them; And God said to them: 'Be fruitful and multiply, and replenish the earth, and subdue it; and have dominion over the fish of the sea, and over the fowl of the air, and over every living thing that creepeth upon the earth.'
>
> (Gen. 1: 28)

In both Genesis accounts, humanity is viewed as the crown of God's creation. Through intelligence and creative energy, people learn to control the earth. They are not entirely subject to the fortunes and failures of nature; and the regular rhythm of the changing seasons is exploited for the growth of crops and the enhancement of life. Though they are physically defenceless, the unique power that is humankind's makes them the match of any animal, but the early chapters of Genesis make it clear that one is not to kill God's creatures.

> And God said: 'Behold, I have given you every herb yielding seed, which is upon the face of all the earth, and every tree, in which is the fruit of a tree yielding seed – to you it shall be for food.'
>
> (Gen. 1: 29)

In the second account, God sets *adam* in the Garden of Eden to 'dress it and keep it' (Gen. 2: 15). As well as the pinnacle of creation, humanity here becomes a partner with God in the maintenance of that creation. God's continued presence is required to prevent the world returning to chaos, but humankind's involvement determines what kind of a world it becomes.

Humanity's purpose is to work.

> 'For the Lord thy God hath blessed thee in all the work of thy hand'. (Deut. 2: 7) . . . If man does work, he receives the divine blessing; if not, he loses it.
>
> (*Midrash* to Psalm 22)

In this passage, work is taken literally, and God's blessing upon humanity is dependent upon this. But in many texts, work means more than physical labour.

> The Holy One, blessed be He, said to him: 'Up to now, I alone was engaged in work, now you too must also be engaged in it.'
>
> (*Zohar Hadash* on Gen. 5)

This mystical text understands work as mirroring God's activity. Humanity's acts of kindness and compassion are as necessary to the world's continued existence as is the tending of the plants in the garden.

Other passages include the worship of God as part of this maintenance plan, based on Isaiah 43: 2, which says: 'This people I formed for myself that they might tell my praise'. Above all, humanity's purpose is to do God's will as expressed in the biblical commandments.

Free will

> In a supreme act of self-limitation, the Absolute God gave man freedom of moral choice. He could will to do right and wrong, obey or disobey his maker. It was heaven's greatest gift to man, he was not an automaton.[7]

This freedom of humanity to act independently of God has often puzzled philosophers, for how does this coincide with God's omnipotence? Today, after the experience of the Holocaust, there is a tendency to move towards a view of the limited power of God, but though the question was addressed by the early rabbis, such a view was out of the question. The problem of reconciling free will with determinism was discussed but never fully resolved. 'All is forseen, yet free choice is granted man' (*Pirkei Avot* 3: 19), remains the classic formulation. The two elements stand side by side, without any attempt to reconcile them. The statement continues: 'The world is judged by goodness, yet all depends on the abundance of work.' (*Pirkei Avot* 3: 19). It was accepted that God was in full control, but the preoccupation of the rabbis was with what God required human beings to do – to exercise free will for the good of the world.

Goodness is one of humanity's basic qualities. At the close of the sixth day of creation God, 'saw everything that he had made and behold, it was very good' (Gen. 1: 31). A person's duty is to maintain this, yet it is possible to choose to refrain from doing so. In the Talmud, *Niddah* 16b, it is said that before conception, the sperm is laid before God who decrees all its qualities except one.

> 'Sovereign of the universe, What shall be the fate of this drop? Shall it produce a strong man or a weak man, a wise man or a fool, a rich man or a poor man?' Whereas 'wicked man' or 'righteous one' he does not

> mention, in agreement with the statement of R. Hanina. For R. Hanina stated: 'Everything is in the hands of God except the fear of God.'

Humanity can, through exercising the moral choice for good, fulfil its destiny as the crown of God's creation; or, through exercising the choice for bad, sink to the level of the animals among whom human beings were formed.

The Garden of Eden

> And the Lord God commanded the man, saying: 'Of every tree of the garden, thou mayest freely eat; but of the tree of the knowledge of good and evil thou shalt not eat of it; for in the day that thou eatest thereof thou shalt surely die'.

The freedom of humanity to disobey was exercised for the first time in the Garden of Eden. Adam ate of the fruit, and guilt, suffering and death were its consequences. Although all humanity is a victim of those consequences, the notion that all people have been tainted by that first wrongful act is not part of Judaism.

There is no idea of 'original sin' – rather, Adam and Eve stand as a paradigm for what happens to each person in his or her life. Every individual stands independently in relationship with God, with the same injunction to obey his commands and the very same possibility to disobey.

> The soul that sinneth it shall die. The son shall not bear the iniquity of the father with him, neither shall the father bear the iniquity of the son with him; the righteousness of the righteous shall be upon him and the wickedness of the wicked shall be upon him.
>
> (Ezek. 18: 20)

What did change with this act were the circumstances in which humanity lives. Eating of the fruit brought knowledge of good and evil, right and wrong. Moral choice was extended beyond that of obedience and disobedience; a fully-fledged sense of ethical conduct now comes into play. Whereas at creation, *adam* was given wisdom – *hokhmah* – and understanding – *binah* – he now acquires knowledge – *daat*.

This knowledge, coupled with freedom of choice, results in great power – for evil as well as for good. To limit this now dangerous power, *adam* is denied access to the tree of life and the possibility of immortality. A new element impedes the divine injunction to work – that of drudgery. Pain is introduced – life will never be the same again.

The medieval philosophers understood the tale allegorically. Moses Maimonides,[8] for example, saw the tree of life as embodying pure wisdom, and the tree of knowledge as practical wisdom. Adam, who was the embodiment of intellectual perfection, chose to follow his instincts rather than pure reason. He gave up the pursuit of facts for that of values; of truth and falsehood for good and evil; of physics and metaphysics for ethics and politics. Other philosophers consider that it is the gross animal nature of humankind that let Adam down. Capable of the highest intellectual perfection, he chose to gratify his senses instead.

But despite the gloominess of this view of humanity, there is always a chance to go back to the golden age of Eden. Humankind, who through folly was driven out, by virtue, can return. Eden is paradise – the walled garden containing the delights of heaven and awaiting the righteous who will enter it after death.

Modern philosophers tend towards a different track, however. While on one level the story seems to be an aetiological myth that harks back to a golden era lost to humanity, on another, there is something strangely positive about it. The childhood of Eden is replaced by the adulthood of life outside the garden. A harder life, true, but one with infinitely greater possibilities – greater potential for good, and for personal and universal fulfilment. This gives rise to the question whether God actually wanted Adam to disobey him. 'Did he fall or was he pushed?' is a recurring question.

Origin and nature of evil

The problem of evil in the world is one that has occupied Jewish thinkers from the Bible onwards. While the Torah emphasises the message: 'Do good and prosper; do evil and suffer', the reality has always been very different. The question of suffering of the righteous arises in the story of Abraham and Sodom (Gen. 18: 23–33), and runs throughout the Prophets and Writings, culminating in the story of Job. It has also dominated the thought of generations of rabbis and remains, even today, one of the major philosophical issues.

The rabbis of the first centuries of the current era lived in a world where dualism was a popular philosophy. Since this threatened the unity of God, they were at pains to emphasise that God was the source of evil, as described in Isaiah:

> I form the light, and create darkness;
> I make peace and create evil;
> I am the Lord, that doeth all these things. (45: 7)

But this is not to mean that God is himself evil, rather, that he creates evil for the world.

Satan appears quite frequently in the Hebrew Bible, and is regarded as an agent of God. The word means 'adversary' and is descriptive of a job, rather than a personality. God's angels perform this function when necessary, for example, in the story of Job where, in order to show the extent of his loyalty to God, it is necessary that Job suffer.

Later Judaism developed an elaborate demonology, and in particular the notion of fallen angels, but the emphasis on God's unity remained so strong that it appears even these remain, to a certain extent, in his power.

Whether God physically created evil or, as other texts suggest, simply allowed evil to exist, it is somehow considered necessary to the world. The early rabbis described humanity as having two desires or inclinations: a good – *yezer ha-tov* – and an evil – *yezer ha-ra*. These are constantly in juxtaposition, and human inconsistency is seen as the result of one or the other momentarily gaining the upper hand. Nevertheless, the *yezer ha-ra* is much the stronger, and a person's life is a constant battle against it.

> R. Isaac stated, 'The [Evil] Inclination of a man grows stronger within him from day to day as it is said, "Only evil all the day." (Gen. 6: 5)'. R. Simeon b. Lakish stated, 'The Evil Inclination grows in strength from day to day and seeks to kill him as it is said, "The wicked watches the righteous and seeketh to slay him" (Ps. 37: 32); and were it not that the Holy One, blessed be He, is his help, he would not be able to withstand it . . .'
>
> (B. Talmud *Sukkah* 52a–b)

The *yezer ha-ra* is variously identified with the sexual instinct, physical appetite, aggression and ambition. However, of itself, it is not altogether evil. *Bereshit Rabbah* 9: 7 suggests:

> But for the Evil Desire, no man would build a house, take a wife and beget children; and thus said Solomon; 'Again I considered all labour and all excelling in work, that it is a man's rivalry with his neighbour.'
>
> (Eccles. 4: 4)

There is a legend that the Men of the Great Assembly[9] once caught the *yezer ha-ra* and were about to put it to death when God intervened saying that if there were no evil inclination, the world itself would die.

But necessary though it may be to the world, it must be overcome in humanity. Each individual must engage in a constant and continuing struggle to overcome the evil inclination that will last throughout life. But the *yezer ha-ra* can be overcome through obedience to God's will.

> In the time to come, the Holy One, blessed be He will bring the Evil Inclination and slay it in the presence of the righteous and the wicked. To the righteous, it will have the appearance of a towering hill, and to the wicked it will have the appearance of a hair thread. Both the former and the latter will weep; the righteous will weep saying, 'How were we able to overcome such a towering hill!' The wicked also will weep saying, 'How is it that we were unable to conquer this hair thread!'
>
> (Babylonian Talmud *Sukkah* 52a)

Sin and wrongdoing

The result of the *yezer ha-ra* gaining control is that humankind sins. In the Bible there are about twenty different words for 'sin', each of which applies to different types of wrongdoing. The most popular are the three *het*, *pesha* and *avon*. They are often used together – as among God's attributes in Exodus 34: 7 – but they have distinctive meanings nevertheless.

The word *het* comes from a Hebrew root meaning to miss the mark, and so comes to mean 'to fail'. It is used in the Bible to signify the failure of relations between two individuals, for example, between Jacob and Laban (Gen. 31: 36), and also the failure in obligation to God, for example, the infringement of the ban (Deut. 20: 16 ff.) in Joshua 7: 11. It is often translated as 'offence' or 'transgression'.

Pesha means 'breach' and suggests a more deliberate act of disobedience. Though used occasionally for relations between individuals, it is more usually associated with humankind's reaction to God's demands, for example, Amos 2: 4. This is the word most usually translated as 'sin', but 'disobedience' or 'rebellion' are closer to the meaning.

The root of the word *avon* means crooked or bent. It suggests some deviation from the good but not necessarily deliberate; rather it is part of the human condition that we should strive against, for example, Psalm 38: 7. Translated traditionally as 'iniquity', the term 'wrong' or 'wrongdoing' fits well here.

For the Bible the main concern with these faults is that they break the special relationship God has with humanity. When persons do wrong, they fail to honour their part of the bargain made with God, known as the covenant, and the fear is that God, in response, will stop helping and protecting his people.

> And it shall come to pass, when thou shalt tell this people all these words, and they shall say unto thee: 'Wherefore hath the Lord pronounced all this great evil against us? or what is our iniquity? or what is our sin that we have committed against the Lord our God?' then shalt thou say unto them: 'Because your fathers have forsaken Me, saith the Lord, and have walked after other gods and have served them, and have worshipped them, and have forsaken Me, and have not kept My law; and ye have done worse than your fathers; for, behold ye walk every one after the stubbornness of his evil heart, so that ye hearken not unto Me'.
>
> (Jer. 16: 10–12)

On the whole, though not entirely, the Bible is concerned with the sins of Israel as a people. Individual responsibility, and concern for individual sin and how it affects society, were ideas developed by the early rabbis. The Mishnah and Talmud[10] are full of discussions on what exactly constitutes sin, its effects, its punishment, and the possibility and means of forgiveness.

The term favoured by the rabbis for sin is *avera*, which comes from a root meaning to pass over, and suggests ignoring or rejecting God's will. Sins were divided into two categories: sins of omission and sins of commission – the latter being the more serious. The rabbis also distinguished between 'light' and 'heavy' sins, recognising that in some circumstances, some of the lighter precepts could be transgressed – in fact should be, to save life, for example. But three sins were considered so serious that people must lose their own life rather than commit them. These were murder, idolatry and sexual crimes such as incest and adultery.

The rabbis carefully delineated the various punishments for sin, but rather than punishment, what God desires most of all is the repentance of the sinner.

> But if the wicked turn from all his sins that he hath committed and keep all My statutes and do that which is lawful and right he shall surely live, he shall not die. None of his transgressions that he hath committed shall be remembered against him; for his righteousness that he hath done he shall live. Have I any pleasure at all that the wicked should die? saith the Lord God; and not rather that he should return from his ways and live?
>
> (Ezek. 18: 21–3)

Repentance and atonement

If sin is seen as turning away from God, either by deliberately breaking his laws, or by default because of humankind's inherent weakness, then repentance is the turning back to him. In the Bible the word used is *shuv* or 'turn' – the turning of the heart or mind back towards God in a new relationship with him. In rabbinic literature, this becomes *teshuvah* – returning – coming back to God and restoring the bond between them. The importance of *teshuvah* is seen in a famous passage, where a lower scriptural authority is overridden by a higher one until the words of God himself override them all.

> They asked of wisdom; What is the punishment of the sinner? Wisdom replied; 'Evil pursues the sinner' (Prov. 13: 21). They asked of prophecy:

> What is the punishment of the sinner? Prophecy replied: 'The soul that sinneth, it shall die' (Ezek. 18: 4). They asked of Torah; What is the punishment of the sinner? Torah replied; 'Let him bring a sacrifice and it will atone.' Then they asked of the Holy One, Blessed be He; What is the punishment of the sinner? He replied, let him repent and bring atonement.
>
> (Jerusalem Talmud *Makkot* 2: 6)

All people can do *teshuvah*. No sin is so great that penitence is impossible, and God will help all he can in the process.

> A king had a son who had gone astray from his father a journey of a hundred days: his friends said to him, 'Return to your father'; he said, 'I cannot'. Then his father sent to say, 'Return as far as you can, and I will come to you the rest of the way'. So God says, 'Return to Me and I will return to you'.
>
> (*Pesikta Rabati*)

Originally, repentance required a public confession of the sin and a sacrifice; later, fasting and prayer replaced the sacrificial element. If the wrong is against a person, the wrongdoer must confess and ask forgiveness of that person as well as make restitution, and resolve never to commit the same offence again. Then the wrongdoer can approach God and the wrong will be pardoned – literally 'covered over' in the Hebrew. It is then as if the sin had never been committed, the slate has been wiped clean. For sins against God, the same process of confession, restitution and resolve never to do the wrong again are involved.

Teshuvah can be made at any time:

> R. Eliezer said: Repent one day before you die. His disciples said, 'Who knows when he will die?' 'All the more, then, let him repent today, for peradventure he will die tomorrow. The result will be that all his life will be spent in penitence.'
>
> (*Midrash* on Psalm 90: 12)

However, the weeks leading up to the Day of Atonement – *Yom Kippur* – are the main period for repentance, with an elaborate liturgy to assist in the process. It begins in the month preceding the

New Year with *selihot* prayers requesting God's pardon. The New Year – *Rosh Hashanah* – is known as the Day of Judgement. On this day, one popular image has it, God looks into the deeds of humankind in the past year and passes judgement. Those who have been totally good are inscribed in the Book of Life, while those who have been thoroughly wicked are inscribed in the Book of Death. For those – the majority – who have been neither completely good nor bad, God suspends judgement until *Yom Kippur* some ten days later. Those Ten Days of Penitence are the time when Jews are expected to repent of their wrongs in order to be granted atonement.

The confession is central to the *Yom Kippur* service. At the time of the Temple and its sacrificial cult, the High Priest would confess on behalf of himself and his family, then for the priesthood, and, finally, for all Israel. Since the destruction of the Temple, each individual Jew confesses for himself or herself, but within the communality of the people of Israel. Thus the public confession that is made repeatedly during the day is for crimes that may not have been committed by the individuals concerned. Nevertheless, through this, it is understood that God forgives his people – till the next time.

The covenant

The history of the world, and particularly of the Jewish people, is perceived through the Bible as one of a constant cycle of wrongdoing, repentance and forgiveness. After Adam, humanity quickly descended into the depths of corruption and violence. Saved through Noah from total destruction, it soon returned to evil. Then one man, Abraham, and the nation that he founded, Israel, became the agents of God's design on earth. Constantly rebelling, refusing to obey God's dictates, this nation suffers punishment, and exile. Restoration and forgiveness come only when they change their ways and return to God.

The idea of a covenant – an agreement between God and individual human beings or nations of help and obligation, and sealed by a sign, or ceremony – is central to Jewish understanding of humankind's relationship with God. The first covenant in the Bible is that made with Noah (Gen. 9: 8–17) and with all living creatures, swearing he will never again wreak such total destruction as wrought by the flood. The sign is the rainbow, and the implication is that human beings, in return, must live better lives than before.

However, humanity continues much as before, and this leads to the choosing of one man rather than all humankind for the furtherance of God's purpose on earth. That man is Abraham, and the covenants made with him (Gen. 15, 17) relate to the giving of land – the land of Israel – and the promise of fathering a great nation. The reciprocal obligation, on the part of Abraham's descendants, is to circumcise their sons on the eighth day after birth, as a sign of the relationship between God and his people.

The covenant that is central to Judaism, however, is that made with Moses on behalf of the people of Israel on Mount Sinai (Exod. 19–24: 11). There, God established himself as the only God of Israel, and Israel became his special people, mutually bound in a series of intricate laws and obligations that are developed through the rest of the Torah, are expanded in rabbinic literature, and have become the overriding focus of Jewish practice to this day.

> If ye walk in my statutes, and keep my commandments, and do them; then I will give you rains in their seasons, and the land shall produce, and the trees of the field shall yield their fruit. And your threshing shall reach unto the vintage, and the vintage shall reach unto the sowing time; and ye shall eat your bread till you have enough, and dwell in your land safely. . . And I will set my tabernacle among you and my soul shall not abhor you. And I will walk among you and will be your God, and ye shall be my people.
>
> (Lev. 26: 3–5, 11–12)

The covenant clearly establishes God as Israel's King. As his subjects, his people not only owe him sole allegiance, but are obligated to behave as fitting representatives of their Lord.

> Now, therefore, if ye hearken to my voice indeed, and keep my covenant, then ye shall be mine own treasure from among all peoples; for all the earth is mine: and ye shall be unto me a kingdom of priests and a holy nation.
>
> (Exod. 19: 5–6)

If Israel fails to keep God's commands, then appropriate punishment follows, seen largely in the barrenness of the land, its conquest, and ultimately the exile of its people.

The rest of the biblical narratives demonstrate how easily Israel fell into breaking the covenant, in particular, in the worship of other gods. The major events of Israelite history, namely, the destruction of the two Temples and the two exiles that followed[11] are understood to be the result of God's response – by breaking his obligation to provide the people with the land of Israel. The prophets look to a future age, however, and a new covenant:

> This is the covenant that I will make with the house of Israel after those days, saith the Lord, I will put my law in their inward parts, and in their heart I will write it; and I will be their God, and they shall be my people; and they shall teach no more every man his brother, saying: 'Know the Lord'; for they shall all know me, from the least of them to the greatest of them, saith the Lord, for I will forgive their iniquity, and their sin I will remember no more.
>
> (Jer. 31: 33–4)

Later Judaism perceived that this will happen with the coming of the Messiah, and the people of Israel will finally be restored in perfect covenant with their God.

The chosen people

Inextricably bound up with the idea of covenant, is that of Israel's election by God to be his special representative on earth.

While in biblical times many tribes would have their particular god, such a relationship would be a natural one without the complications of theology. There was no idea of a god choosing his particular people. Yet God's specific choosing of Israel is central to Jewish theology. Moreover, the choice was reciprocal.

> And Joshua said unto the people: 'Ye are witnesses against yourselves that ye have chosen you the Lord to serve Him'. – And they said: 'We are witnesses'.
>
> (Jos. 24: 22)

Another difference for Israel was that their god was the God of all peoples, and the obligation on the part of Israel was towards all nations.

> Thus sayeth God the Lord, He that created the heavens and stretched them forth, He that spread forth the earth and that which cometh out of it, He that giveth breath unto the people upon it, And spirit to them that walk therein: I the Lord have called thee in righteousness, And have taken hold of thy hand, And kept thee, and set thee for a covenant of the people, For a light of the nations; To open the blind eyes, To bring out the prisoners from the dungeon, And them that sit in darkness out of the prison house.
>
> (Isa. 42: 5–7)

In a strange way, the particularism of the notion of a chosen people gives rise to a universalism of vision. God chooses his people to serve his purpose in the further destiny of all humanity. By following God's commandments – *mitzvot* – Israel is contributing to the perfecting of the world.

> By three things is the world sustained: by the Law, by the Temple service, and by deeds of loving kindness.
>
> (*Pirkei Avot* 1: 2)

This, probably the most famous passage in the Mishnah, attributed to Simeon the Just,[12] indicates the centrality of this notion. Of the three things essential to the maintenance of the world, two are exclusively Jewish activities, while the third, though a universal principle, is clear in this context to refer to Jewish obligation only.

The people of Israel were also required to witness to God's nature and being in the universe. Through them the world would turn to God. This did not mean converting to Judaism, but turning to the worship of the one true God. Many today would claim this to have happened through the spread of Christianity and Islam – two religions that owe their roots to Judaism. So in this way, too, the particularism of the chosenness of Israel can be seen as leading to universalism.

Nevertheless, through the centuries there has been some considerable embarrassment at what appears to be an exclusivistic view of the nature of the universe and humankind's place in it. The medieval rabbis were at pains to stress that Israel was chosen for service, not privilege, and that greater responsibility lay upon the Jew, therefore, than the non-Jew. The Jew had to observe all the commandments, or *mitzvot*, of the Torah – calculated as 613 – while the non-Jew had to observe only seven to be accounted a righteous person. These seven are known as the *mitzvot* of the sons of Noah, harking back to the Noachide covenant, and are usually understood to relate to idolatry, blasphemy, sexual sins, murder, theft, eating a limb from a living animal and establishing courts of justice. Moreover, the greater responsibility of Israel meant the greater the punishment for erring: 'You only have I known of all the families of the earth; Therefore I will visit upon you all your iniquities' (Amos 3: 2).

Finally, the rabbis found some justification for Israel's chosenness in the notion that other nations had been selected first, but refused to accept the role.

> Before God gave Israel the Torah, He approached every tribe and nation, and offered them the Torah, that hereafter they might have no excuse to say, 'Had the Holy One, blessed be He, desired to give us the Torah, we should have accepted it'. He went to the children of Esau and said, 'Will ye accept the Torah?' They answered Him, saying, 'What is written therein?' He answered them, 'Thou shalt not kill.' Then they all said: 'Wilt Thou perchance take from us the blessing with which our Father Esau was blessed? For he was blessed with the words, "By thy sword shalt thou live." We do not want to accept the Torah.' Thereupon He went to the children of Lot and said unto them, 'Will ye accept the Torah?' They said 'What is written therein?' He answered, 'Thou shalt not commit unchastity.' They said, 'From unchastity we spring; we do not want to accept the Torah.' Then He went to the children of Ishmael and said: 'Do ye want to accept the Torah?' They said 'What is written therein?' He answered, 'Thou shalt not steal.' They said, 'Wilt Thou take from us the blessing with which our father was blessed? God promised him "His hand will be against every man." We do not want to accept Thy Torah.' Thence he went to all the other nations, who likewise rejected the Torah saying: 'We cannot give up the law of our fathers, we do not want Thy Torah, give it to Thy people Israel.' Upon this, he came to Israel and spoke to them, 'Will ye accept the Torah?' They said to him, 'What is written therein?' He answered, 'Six hundred and thirteen commandments.' They said, 'All that the Lord has spoken, we will do and be obedient.'[13]

While embarrassment with the notion of Israel's election continues to exist, there is no sign that the idea will ever lose its central importance. Jewish prayers are full of references to it, for example, in the sanctification of a Festival.

> Blessed art Thou, O Lord, our God, King of the Universe, who has chosen us from among all peoples and exalted us above all nations and hallowed us by Thy commandments.[14]

However, although Israel may be perceived as the agents of God in the world, the ultimate redemption that is expected will extend to all peoples.

Messiah

Redemption will come in the Messianic Age – a future era when the world be perfected and all humanity will come to know God. While Judaism allows for the possible perfection of humanity by itself, there exists alongside that, a notion of a future divine intervention in the world that will stop the bloodshed and restore the world's people to the state of bliss that was theirs in the Garden of Eden.

The Bible contains both ideas. The prophets Nahum, Habakkuk, Malachi and Joel describe a messianic age brought about by the people's change of heart, while Isaiah, Micah, Jeremiah and Zechariah look to a messianic figure who will be the ideal leader, executing justice and righteousness in the name of the Lord, once he has redeemed his people.

> And a throne is established through mercy,
> And there sitteth thereon in truth, in the tent of David,
> One that judgeth, and seeketh justice, and is
> ready in righteousness.
>
> (Isa. 6: 5)

Depending on the period in history, or the particular circumstances of the period, either one or the other idea has been the more popular.

The term 'messiah' comes from a Hebrew word meaning to anoint. In the Bible, kings and high priests are anointed with oil to indicate divine sanction of their office. One non-Jewish King is also called messiah; that is Cyrus, the Persian ruler who allowed the return to Jerusalem of the exiled Jews in Babylonia (Isa. 45: 1). He fulfils the function of messiah in that he acts as an agent of God, carrying out his divine purpose.

The apocalyptic literature of the centuries that followed the Prophets developed an elaborate plan of exactly how the messianic age would come about. This included miraculous 'signs'; cataclysmic events, such as earthquakes, wars, famine and floods known as the 'birthpangs of the Messiah'; the return of Elijah, who, according to biblical tradition, never died (2 Kgs 2: 11), and, according to later tradition, would announce the imminent arrival of the Messiah; the 'trumpet of the Messiah' – the blowing of the heavenly *shofar* as at the revelation on Mount Sinai (Exod. 19: 19); the 'ingathering of the exiles', when all Jews will return to the promised land; the reception of proselytes; the final apocalyptic war between the forces of good and evil – 'the war of Gog and Magog' (Ezek. 38–9); the 'Days of the Messiah', when he rules the earth with righteousness (Isa. 9: 1–6 and others); the renovation of the world, where it is restored to its original pristine glory; The Day of Judgement; the bodily Resurrection of the Dead; and finally, the World to Come.

All these ideas had an enormous effect on subsequent literature, though nothing like a fixed and totally-accepted doctrine ever emerged. Some rabbis concentrated on trying to calculate the time of the Messiah's arrival, others on his identity, others on the qualities the Messiah would show.

Over the centuries, at times of great persecution, messianic figures have arisen, only to be regarded, after their failure to materially change the world, as false messiahs. In our age, the Lubavitch Hasidim[15] declare that their leader, or 'Rebbe', is the Messiah, but that it is up to the Jews of the world to observe Judaism correctly, before he will reveal himself.

This theory connects that of divine intervention with the idea of human ability and responsibility to perfect the world. Hasidic theology is based on that of the sixteenth-century kabbalists, and in particular Isaac Luria,[16] who proposed the notion of the divine sparks. According to this doctrine, the divine light that emanated from the Godhead was too strong to be contained in the lower reaches of the heavens, and by some cosmic catastrophe, the vessels that held it shattered, and the light fell as sparks to earth. To effect the repair of the cosmos, it becomes the duty of the Jew to lift up those sparks and restore them to heaven, through piety and observance of the *mitzvot*. In this view, humanity can redeem not only itself and the world, but also the entire cosmos, and even the Godhead itself, by its own efforts alone.

The main champion of a messianic age without a messiah is Progressive Judaism.[17] Influenced by the belief prevalent in the early decades of this century, that humanity was indeed moving into a new era of peace and universal friendship, it rejected the notion of a personal messiah in favour of a messianic age, based on the writings of the Prophets. Though this optimism was shattered by the Holocaust and has resulted in a reappraisal, the majority of Progressive Jews still believe humanity can, by its own efforts, change the world. If God intervenes at all, it is by changing the hearts of human beings, not by sending a leader or by miraculous or apocalyptic events.

After death

The idea of an existence after death is central to Jewish belief, though again, there is no one consistent idea found in the various developments of Jewish thought.

The Bible has no clear description of what life after death is like, though references to *Sheol* – a dark, shadowy underworld – run through the prophetic books, most notably in the story concerning Saul and the witch of En Dor in 1 Samuel 28: 8. It has been suggested that this was part of a popularist faith that was frowned upon by the religious authorities as being part of pagan culture.

The one biblical passage upon which the beliefs of later Judaism seem to be based is that of Daniel 12: 2.

> And many of them that sleep in the dust of the earth shall awake, some to everlasting life, and some to reproaches and everlasting abhorrence.

Alongside the notion of a messiah, during the time of the Second Temple two distinctive ideas emerged: the immortality of the soul, and the bodily resurrection of the dead. The problem is that they are in some sense contradictory and much of rabbinic literature on the subject is, therefore, inconsistent.

> R. Jacob said: This world is like a vestibule before the world to come: prepare thyself in the vestibule that thou mayest enter into the banqueting hall.
>
> (*Pirkei Avot* 4: 16)

It is not clear whether the world to come is to be enjoyed on earth, or in heaven. The ideas expressed in rabbinic literature suggest the following sequence. On death the soul leaves the body and remains for a year in *Sheol* as a sort of purgatory. Then the wicked enter *Gehinnon* where they suffer unremitting punishment, while the righteous enter into the delights of the Garden of Eden, a place where the sages of all generations discuss scripture while their wives sit at their feet. With the coming of the Messiah, comes universal redemption; the souls return to dust where they are reconstituted with their bodies, and the righteous enter the world to come where:

> there is no eating nor drinking nor propagation nor business nor jealousy nor hatred nor competition, but the righteous sit with their crowns on their heads feasting on the brightness of the divine presence.
>
> (B. Talmud *Berakhot* 17a)

The medieval philosophers were concerned by the contradictions and tried hard to resolve them. Saadia Gaon did so by implying two resurrections and suggesting that punishment for the wicked was eternal. Moses Maimonides virtually ignored the idea of a physical resurrection, putting forward the idea of the soul's immortality in the active intellect, with heavenly bliss as the knowledge of God and *Gehinnon* as the annihilation of the soul. Kabbalistic mysticism took yet another idea found in rabbinic Judaism, that of *gilgul* or the transmigration of souls, to suggest that the sinner is one that has not fulfilled its soul's destiny and that soul must return in other bodies till such time as it does so.

While it appears that, theologically, the idea of the immortality of the soul took precedence over that of resurrection, in popular religion, where it was (mistakenly) perceived as being more authentically Jewish, resurrection became the overriding belief. The few sentences that Maimonides wrote on resurrection became a Principle of Faith[18] while his lengthy treatises on the soul are ignored.

The main prayer of Judaism, the Eighteen Benedictions, or *Amidah*, contains the following paragraph.

> Thou sustainest the living with lovingkindness, revivest the dead with great mercy, supportest the falling, healest the sick, freest the bound, and keepest thy faith with them that sleep in the dust. Who is like unto thee, Lord of mighty acts, and who resembleth thee, O King, who orderest death and restorest life and causest salvation to spring forth? Yea, faithful thou art to revive the dead. Blessed art thou, O lord who revivest the dead.[19]

This prayer, which owes its origins to the Pharisees who were in conflict with the Sadducees over this matter, is said three times daily – four times on Sabbaths and Festivals. So the belief is still strongly present in Judaism although, today, many deny its literal import. The current trend seems not to speculate, but to say, with Maimonides, that to try to grasp the nature of the hereafter is 'like a man who is blind trying to grasp the nature of colour'.[20]

NOTES

1. Homiletical interpretations of the Bible composed by rabbis in the early centuries of the current era.
2. Quoted in Isidore Epstein, *The Faith of Judaism*, Soncino Press, London, 1954, p. 210.
3. Babylonia, 882–942 CE, one of the greatest and most influential Jewish thinkers.
4. *Bereshit Rabbah* 8: 1.
5. *Alphabet of Ben Sira* c. tenth century CE.
6. 'Eminence does not become a woman. There were two eminent women in the Bible . . . their names are hateful' (Deborah means hornet, and Hulda, weasel.), Babylonian Talmud, *Megillah* 14a.
7. Steven T. Katz, *Jewish Ideas and Concepts*, Schocken Books, New York, 1977, p. 102.
8. 1135–1204 b. Spain. Foremost philosopher combining Aristotelian principles with classic Jewish teaching.

9. Leaders of Israel during the Persian period from Ezra to 'Simeon the Just' (probably the High Priest Simeon II, 219–199 BCE).
10. Mishnah: codification of rabbinic law compiled in Palestine 200 CE. Talmud: rabbinic commentaries on the Mishnah, written in Palestine and Babylon c. third–sixth century.
11. 586 BCE followed by the Babylonian exile, and 70 CE by the Romans, followed by the general dispersion which, despite the establishment of the State of Israel in 1948, is perceived as still continuing.
12. See note 9.
13. Quoted in Ginzberg, *The Legends of the Jews*, Philadelphia, 1968, Vol. III, p. 80.
14. J.H. Hertz, *The Authorised Daily Prayer Book*, London, 1976, p. 808.
15. Hasidism emerged in seventeenth-century Poland as a popularist quasi-mystical sect in reaction to the excessive scholasticism of the rabbinic Judaism of the time. On the death of its founder, the movement organised itself into different sects each following a particular charismatic 'rebbe', of whom today the Lubavitch are the most well known.
16. 1534–1572. The foremost mystic of the most influential school of Kabbalah centred in Safed in Galilee.
17. Following on the enlightenment and the emancipation of the Jews in Europe in the eighteenth century, there was a reformation of Judaism that sought more contemporary interpretations of Jewish tradition in the light of modern secular thinking. In England today, this is represented by two movements: Liberal Judaism and Reform.
18. Maimonides' *Thirteen Principles of Faith*, based on his commentary to Mishnah *Sanhedrin* 10: 1, are printed in all Orthodox prayerbooks, cf. the *Authorised Daily Prayer Book*, p. 248.
19. *Authorised Daily Prayer Book*, p. 135.
20. Moses Maimonides' Commentary on the Mishnah; *Sanhedrin* 10: 1.

FURTHER READING

Cohen, Arthur A. and Mendes-Flohr, Paul (eds), (1987) *Contemporary Jewish Religious Thought*, New York, Charles Scribners.

Cohen, S.S. (1971) *Jewish Theology*, Assen, Royal Vangorum.

Epstein, I. (1954) *The Faith of Judaism*, London, Soncino.

Eisenstein, I. (ed.) (1966) *Varieties of Jewish Belief*, New York, Reconstructionist Press.

Heschel, A.J. (1955) *God in Search of Man*, New York, Jewish Publication Society.

Jacobs, L. (1973) *A Jewish Theology*, London, Darton Longman and Todd.
Kohler, K. (1968) *Jewish Theology*, New York, Ktav.
Schechter, S. (1961) *Aspects of Rabbinic Theology*, New York, Ktav.
Scholem, Gershom G. (1971) *The Messianic Idea in Judaism*, New York, Schocken Books.

Articles in the *Encyclopaedia Judaica* (1972), Jerusalem, Keter Publishing House.

6. Sikhism

Beryl Dhanjal

The *weltbild* (conception of the universe) of the Sikh gurūs was that of the Panjab of their day. They did not re-invent explanations of creation, or feel it necessary to alter understanding of the processes of life and death. The traditional Indian explanations which had stood the test of time were accepted. So, many Sikh beliefs are not very different from the beliefs of the other religions which originated in India.

Creation

The obvious place to start looking for meaning for the human predicament would be the very beginning – creation itself. God created this earth and more. Guru Nanak appreciated the whole of creation, the universe: 'beyond the earth there are more worlds, more and more'. In this creation, there are 'beings of various kinds, colours, and names – He wrote them all with a flowing pen. If anyone knew how to record their number what an immense account it would be!' (*Japjī*: *pauṛi* 16).

The Gurū says that for millions of years there was nothing but darkness and void. Nothing else existed save the one Absolute Lord. Humans do not know when creation began; nor does anyone know the reasons for the creation – these are known only to God himself. In fact, the Sikh Gurūs make it abundantly clear that there are many things which humans do not know and cannot know – and people should not pretend to such knowledge, for to do so is to delude oneself in false, egotistical pride. People genuinely do not know why they are here, why they were created, and why they wander separated from God.

Rebirth

Sikhs believe in reincarnation. They believe that there are beings, both sentient and non-sentient. The sentient being is an immortal *jīva* (a spirit or soul). In common with other Indian religions, Sikhs accept that the soul neither dies nor can it be destroyed. They also believe that this *jīva* is subject to *saṃsāra* (wandering), which means that it constantly comes back to this life and inhabits a series of bodies.

Lives are decided by actions. What individuals sow by their actions in one life, is reaped in the next life. One's deeds earn *karam*, fate or destiny, in line with deeds done in present or past lives.

> Many times I was born as a tree, many times as an animal, many times I came in the form of a snake, and many times I flew as a bird.
>
> Many times did I break into shops in the city, strong buildings, and having burgled them returned home. I looked ahead and behind, but how could it be concealed from Thee? (Gurū Granth Sāhib: 156)

Guru Arjan asks:

> How many births have you spent as a worm or a moth, an elephant, a fish or a deer? In how many births were you a bird or a snake? or yoked as a horse or an ox?
>
> Meet the Lord of the Universe. Now is the time to meet him.
>
> After a long time you have been given a human body.
>
> How many births were you created as rocks and mountains? born as a vegetable? How many times were you aborted from the womb? You wandered through the eighty-four lakhs of forms of existence. (Gurū Granth Sāhib: 176)

Traditionally, it is said that there are eighty-four lakhs of different lives – 8.4 million of them. The *jīva* has been inanimate, existing as a rock and has been all of the low life forms. It has been a plant and all manner of creatures. After a very long time spent in all those other existences, now, as a human being, 'you have finally come to this body'. This is an opportunity not to be missed (Gurū Granth Sāhib: 176).

> Man is born and dies. Where does he come from and where does he go to? How is he bound to the round of coming and going [transmigration] and how does he gain release? How can he be united with the Eternal Lord? He who has the Lord's Name in his heart and on his tongue becomes beyond desire, as the Lord himself is. Man comes and goes [transmigrates]. He is born because of the desires of his mind. The God-minded are freed and not bound again for they dwell on the word and obtain deliverance through the Name.
>
> (Gurū Granth Sāhib: 152)

So humans continue to be reborn because of the desires of their minds, but they can end the cycle by removing these desires through meditating on the Name and becoming God-minded. Human birth, therefore, is that rare opportunity among all those existences – the occasion when the *jīva* can break the pattern and a person can achieve union with God. But 'Those who turn their back on the Gurū are born again as pigs and dogs. Fettered by their evil tendencies, they come and go' (Gurū Granth Sāhib: 832).

We do not know exactly how the process works. The Sikh Gurūs do not specify in detail how the activity system in which we live functions. They do not speculate as to how long *jīva*s spend in various existences, or what decides which existence a person takes next, or even how long elapses between different earthly existences.

In Sikhism, rebirth, *karam*, and *mukti* (liberation from transmigration), are not ultimately important; becoming one with God is all that matters, and this can happen in life. One should concentrate on seeking the beloved to the exclusion of all else. One should not worry about anything else, for getting involved in all such speculation is wasting time and wandering in delusion.

What is it to be human?

First of all, to be human is to have a body. This is important; a body is a very good thing to have:

> The body is the temple of God. In it are revealed precious pearls of knowledge.
>
> (Gurū Granth Sāhib: 1346)

> God is present in the body. The body is his temple. In the body is the place of pilgrimage, of which I am a pilgrim.
>
> (Gurū Granth Sāhib: 659)

If interior religion is of paramount importance, then what happens inside is what matters, not what happens somewhere outside. So a body is necessary. 'I searched and searched within the body, and the Gurū revealed the mystery therein' (Gurū Granth Sāhib: 659). So the body itself is valued: God has created it and he has infused it with light, so there is no yearning to be free of it.

Persons are not apart from God; they do not exist separately just because they are existing on earth in a body. God is still within them, and they are still within God. So the body is not to be viewed as impure, a hindrance, or in any way nasty. It is not in any sense unclean and certainly should not be in a physical sense – Guru Nanak was enthusiastic in recommending the beneficial effects of soap and water.

People should look after their bodies. Many Sikhs take this quite seriously and are very keen on sport and exercise. They like body-building, weightlifting, wrestling, the martial arts, etc., which are designed to strengthen the body and keep it in good condition, and also excel in team games, like hockey, competing successfully at the highest levels in these sports. The hockey teams, martial arts and other sporting activities are organised by gurdwaras and are an important part of their programmes. They hold sports tournaments for the members. Modern Panjabi women also now take part in sport.

Sikhs should not undertake any physical rigours designed to have spiritual ends. They should not push themselves to physical limits or perform the extraordinary feats of physical endurance or austerity practised by some people. They should not beat and torture themselves or mortify their bodies – in short, they should not punish their bodies for any reason. They should look after themselves, eat, drink and keep themselves clean; basically, they should lead normal, happy married lives. A Sikh male should be *gṛhastha*, a householder, have a wife and family, make an honest living and help himself and others. While living very much in the world, he should also seek Truth. There should be no fasting, no celibacy, no austerities. Of course, Sikhs should not go to the other extreme and be vain. The desirable state is one of disciplined worldliness.

FEMALE NATURE

Modern Sikhs claim equality for women, though that is not the same as granting equality. Men fulfil male roles and women fulfil female roles.

Most adjectives and epithets for God are masculine, though occasionally he is referred to as a female, often by using the names of female Indian goddesses. By far the greatest number of references to women in the Gurū Granth Sāhib apply to married women. God is the true husband, and the *man*, (the heart or mind – where decisions are made in a human frame) is the wife, who pines for him. The most usual image of a good wife is very conventional. The poets use the poetic convention, writing as females, yearning for the true master.

> My beloved Lord is not far away. When my soul was reconciled to the word of the Gurū, I found God the prop of my life. In this way the bride met God, the bridegroom, and became his beloved.
>
> (Gurū Granth Sāhib: 473)

If the *man* is a worthy bride, she seeks blessings so that she may attain union with her true husband. She is humble, modest, devoted and obedient, but she dresses and makes herself attractive for him. Conversely, the bad wife has little to recommend her. She is slothful, heedless, faithless and, of course, she is very unfortunate!

On the whole, there is not a great deal written about female nature. Bhai Gurdas said, 'From a temporal and spiritual point of view woman is half man's body and assists him to salvation. She assuredly bringeth happiness to the virtuous' (Bhai Gurdas Vār 5: 16).

Judgement

God created the universe, the busy activity system we all inhabit. This is an important place because it is the one where we have a chance to recognise him and his truth, and where we have a chance to direct our selves toward him. It is a place for doing justice – the court of God – and it is here that we prepare for judgement.

People are judged and the true devotees unite with him, and live with honour and joy in God's realm. Guru Nanak did not discard Indian mythology. He said that in God's court, *Dharmrāj* (i.e. *Yam*, a Vedic deity, the Lord of Death) sings at the gate. Also singing are the two recording angels, *Chitr* and *Gupt*, 'who know how to write' (*Japjī*, *pauṛi* 27). *Dharmrāj* judges individuals on their written records. A phrase commonly used is: 'As he himself soweth, he himself eateth' (*Japjī*, *pauṛi* 20), which places responsibility for the outcome squarely on human shoulders.

According to Sikhism, there is a judgement soon after death. *Jīva*s do not wait until the end of the world and a final judgement; the process is on-going. It is on-going because humans love illusory things. 'So long as man is in love with illusory things, so long shall *Dharmrāj* continue to punish him' (Guru Arjan, *Sukhmaṇī Sāhib Astapadian* 12: 4). The same idea is repeated many times in the Gurū Granth Sāhib. Yet the God of Death is a friend to those who have attained enlightenment through the Word. Humans can conquer death and erase their past actions (Gurū Granth Sāhib: 491, 1091, 698, 614). Judgement, being an on-going process as far as the *jīva* is concerned, consists of the reckoning of the total of the earnings from that life which is being judged. Every action earns *karam*, so when people are judged, they have already sealed their own fate in their lifetime. Guru Nanak said: 'We get hereafter only what we gave out here in honest earnings' (Gurū Granth Sāhib: 472). It is up to human beings to earn the best they can.

Heaven and hells

There are a great many references in Sikh writings to heaven and hell, though these appear to be states and not geographical places. In addition, since they are part of an on-going process, they are not envisaged as lasting – certainly not for all eternity. Even the best of heavens lasts only as long as the merit which earned them lasts, and then the occupants are returned to wander again. Guru Arjan says, 'My heaven is the place where the praises of God are sung' (Gurū Granth Sāhib: 749). Conversely, 'Hell is anywhere where deceit is found' (Gurū Granth Sāhib: 315). 'In the depths of hell there is immense pain. Ungrateful wretches are cast there' (Gurū Granth Sāhib: 315).

Neither heaven nor hell is of as great importance as such concepts are in some other faiths. Guru Nanak said that 'the man who longs for God's abode is unconcerned with heaven and hell' (Gurū Granth Sāhib: 360). In fact, even the traditional Indian goal of *mukti* (liberation, freedom from rebirth) is not ultimately important. The presence of God is more valued. These are merely impermanent states which do not compare with the presence of God. 'Everyone longs for paradise, *mukti* and heaven and rests all hope on them. Those who desire the vision of God do not seek release, they are satisfied and comforted by that sight alone' (Gurū Granth Sāhib: 1324).

Life and death

Life and death are certainly not worth worrying about. As striving for liberation or for paradise is not important, so worrying about living or fearing dying is foolish.

> Because if a man truly loves God, what does he care for salvation or paradise?
>
> I have no anxiety regarding death, and I have no desire for life.
>
> Thou art the cherisher of all living things; our very breathing is taken into account.
>
> Thou dwellest in the body, as it pleases thee, so thou decideth.
>
> O my soul, by uttering God's name, the heart is satisfied.
>
> Under the Guru's instructions, divine knowledge is obtained and the burning of the heart extinguished.
>
> (Gurū Granth Sāhib: 786)

To focus on death and life after death, or even on reincarnation or *mukti* (liberation from further existences), would be to distort Sikh belief and to give a false focus. Death is simply not important; it is as God pleases. At the time of bereavement, Sikhs often say that it is as *Vāhigurū* orders – he knows best. Sikhs are enjoined not to weep and mourn excessively.

Eschatological speculation is foreign to Sikh belief. God may or may not end the world at some point; he is all powerful. 'He does as he likes' (*Asa dī Vār*, *pauṛi* 24). No one can say anything else. The Gurūs often comment that mere people cannot comprehend or describe him, and what he does with creation is his choice. It is not going to make a difference to a person's quest. To speculate about eschatology is to wander in delusion; the goal of this life is union with God.

Society

Although there are references to society in the writings of the Gurūs, they were so intent on their special spiritual message that it took precedence over all other concerns. When Guru Nanak mentions rulers and the conduct of society, he does so to make a spiritual point. But as McLeod (1968: 162–3) observed, 'it is obvious that his teachings have had effects which extend far beyond a recognisably religious context'.

Modern Sikhs do have ideas, and some have expressed them strongly, about how society ought to work and how people ought to behave. The individual ought to contribute to society and not be a burden upon it. Begging is frowned upon. There is nothing to stop people from searching for Truth and doing their duty within society at the same time; the two things are not incompatible and a person should do both.

In fact, Sikhs should try to do a good job at whatever it is they do. A farmer should be a good farmer, and should strive to be a better one and an example to others. A businessman should be successful. A career of any kind ought to be not just a career, but an example of excellence. Positive encouragement towards a profession or career, further education, or self-improvement of some kind, is given by most Sikh families. Nowadays, there is encouragement for girls to embark upon careers too.

A person should not be poor and pursue self-denial; there is no virtue in poverty. A person should be cheerful, optimistic and spirited. Sikhs have an expression, *caṛdi kalā*, which means 'on the up and up' – assertive, in a buoyant mood – and that is how people should be. Being devoted to God is not incompatible with laughing, eating, playing and being well-dressed. When someone said to Guru Hargovind that he did not look much like a holy man, because he dressed like a Prince and went about with an armed retinue, he replied, 'Worldliness without, saintliness within'.

Sikhs have social obligations which they take very seriously, and many of them believe that Sikhism works for the uplift of society as a whole. Many modern Sikhs see Sikhism as egalitarian, casteless, guaranteeing gender equality, democratic, and in tune with modern life and values. Some see it as almost a sort of idealistic socialism. Because that is how they envisage it, that is how they would like to practise it. This does not mean, however, that Sikhs deny the existence of suffering.

SORROW AND SUFFERING

'*Nānak dukhiā sabh sansār*' – 'Oh, Nanak! the whole world is suffering' (Gurū Granth Sāhib: 954). The actual phrase Guru Nanak used has become a proverb, the name of a popular film, and the basis of a popular song. He advised seeking union with God. All sorrow will then be gone. But humans have to accept and submit: 'It is foolish to ask for the gift of joy and the withdrawal of sorrow. Pleasures and pains are the two garments given to man from the court of God' (Gurū Granth Sāhib: 149).

The human state

Despite humans having the opportunity to unite with God, few actually take advantage of the possibilities. Life may be an instrument for spiritual attainment but not everyone actually achieves much in that direction, and so *jīva*s continue to wander. The important part of a human being, inside the body, is the *man* – the mind, the intelligence, the place where decisions are made in the heart. The *man* decides on further wandering or it seeks God. It can either dwell on the Name or it can be the seat of evil impulses; it can take a person to the ultimate, or it can busy itself in greed, deceit and hypocrisy. Only rare people truly love, worship and cleave to God.

Bhai Gurdas, Vār I, says that of all the lakhs of lives, 'the human body is the highest form, because the eyes can see, ears can hear, and the mouth can speak loving words'. To paraphrase his words, persons can work with their hands, can walk and join in the company of believers, can earn by doing their own *dharam*, and feed themselves and give to others. The life of God-attuned persons is successful if they read and understand the *gurbāṇī* and teach it to others. Those who do right will save themselves and others.

Although human beings are marked out as the highest life form, God's little creatures may not be without hope. Guru Nanak did observe that, 'Kings and emperors who have oceans and mountains of wealth are not equal to the little ant who doesn't forget God in her heart'. He also observed, 'On hearing the matters of heaven, even the worms become jealous'. All beings have consciousness: 'None has been created without it. They follow the path according to their understanding. Judged in the same way, they come and go' (Gurū Granth Sāhib: 24).

But being human seems to be the place from which a person stands the best chance of progress and of attaining union with the Lord, perhaps because of the level of understanding. Why then, do people not turn towards the Lord?

MANMUKH

The problem standing in the way is the condition the Gurū described as being *manmukh*. *Man* means the human heart, where decisions are made, and *mukh* means face. Being *manmukh* means facing one's own *man* and, therefore, being self-centred. The reverse and desirable condition is to be *gurmukh*, with the gaze fixed toward the Gurū (not a living person but the True Gurū). Being *manmukh* is not just self-centred in the sense of being selfish; it is far more grave. It is being self-fixated as opposed to being God-centred.

People who are *manmukh* turn towards their own desires and interests. They are full of self-centred pride and their own concerns. They see themselves and not God as the centre of the universe, and seek satisfaction and follow their own designs.

HAUMAI

Haumai, the expression for the wilful disobedience of the *manmukh*, is difficult to translate. *Hau* means 'I' and *mai* also means 'I' – thus *haumai* means 'I, I'. People use words such as ego, egoism, egotism, I-ness, My-ness; Macauliffe (1909) uses 'pride'; and McLeod (1968: 182–3) discusses the various possible translations. It is, basically, an obsession with the self instead of with God. Although the English word 'sin' has particular connotations not really compatible with Sikhism, in this case it may be justifiable to borrow the term. *Haumai* is the condition of McLeod's 'unregenerate man' (1968: 177) – a term which describes well the usual condition of humanity.

Guru Nanak says that in *haumai* a person comes and goes, is born and dies, and goes to heaven and hell. So, wrapped in *haumai* and without the Gurū, 'the man wanders astray, following his own conceit . . . destined for hell and hoping for heaven he remains in the grip of his self-centred pride' (*Asa dī Vār*, *pauṛi* 14). Such people do not know the value of deliverance, and are born and reborn because of their actions. When they understand their own self-centred condition, then they will be able to find the door.

People who are *manmukh* are unaware of truth, reality and God. They are trapped in their own *man*, seeing only what they themselves project, which is their own deluding *māyā*. They work on a basis of individuality, which separates them from the rest of life, the world, the creation and God.

Preservation of the self becomes the struggle, and, struggling to exist, they become assertive, selfish, proud and self-seeking. This sort of attitude, this pattern of living, can never be a help. It has to be rooted out. This may be rather difficult for those from a western culture to appreciate, where individuality is respected and assertiveness taught.

Wrongdoing

Most religions are concerned with the existence of wrongdoing, or at least consider the nature of the human predicament. The human predicament, failings and weaknesses stem basically from the fact that humanity is *manmukh* and deludes itself. Wrongdoing therefore comes from being *manmukh* and not *gurmukh*. So long as the *man* is busy with its own petty concerns, busying itself in its individuality and separation from God, so long will its wrongdoing continue.

The worst evil impulses are the 'five enemies', which were frequently denounced by the Gurū. These are stumbling blocks which lie in the path and have to be dealt with in order to progress. They are lust, anger, envy and covetousness, attachment to worldly things, and pride. All violence and falsehood stem from these enemies and that is why they must be vanquished.

There is also a list of five virtues, but, as Macauliffe (1909) observed, these lists are somewhat arbitrary. The virtues usually mentioned include truth, contentment, compassion, piety, patience and morality (some say that self-control, forgiveness, love of God and humility should also be included). Contentment is always high on the list. It is worth considering these vices and virtues because they are the basis of a good deal of popular religion. Plain folk, busy with their everyday work, perhaps not able to spend time on matters spiritual, would think people ought to be content, patient, etc.

MĀYĀ

The *manmukh* is deluded by *māyā*, which for Guru Nanak does not mean cosmic illusion. Although many of the terms used in Sikhism are similar to, or even the same as, the words used in other Indian religions, the words do not necessarily mean quite the same thing. The creation is God's and is real; not True in the sense that he is True, because the creation may be transitory and only he is True and eternal, but the creation is real enough and not *māyā*. This *māyā* is self-delusion. People who are *manmukh* stand in their own way. They decide their own fate because they submit to their own selves and do not look to the Gurū. Being caught in *māyā*, a person responds to the world and not to the Lord.

Hukam

To be guilty of *haumai*, to be set upon the self, is to waste one's existence. How then is 'the Truth to be attained, the veil of falsehood to be broken'? By walking according to the *hukam*, 'the will of God, as preordained' (*Japjī*, *pauṛi* 1).

Human beings should observe and submit to the *hukam*. The *hukam* means God's order, and, similar to the Christian concept, means both God's order, his commandments, and also the rules which lie behind the universe. These things are all the will of God. God's will underlies everything that happens. All joys, sorrows, suffering, liberation, transmigrations, destiny – everything comes by his order.

The devotee has to recognise this, to submit, and to live according to the *hukam* without complaint. A person who is in the clutches of *haumai* walks in opposition to the *hukam*, self-willed and lost. God is inscrutable. He works in his own ways which humans cannot understand. The devotee has to be unswerving in the faith that God is altogether good and merciful, and that there is a purpose behind everything: 'All are subject to the order. No one is outside it' (*Japjī, pauṛi* 2).

> All forms are created by the *Hukam*. The *Hukam* can not be described. Through the *Hukam*, living beings are created, by his order they achieve greatness.
>
> By the *Hukam* some are exalted and others are laid low. They suffer joy and pain according to the *Hukam*.
>
> Everything and everybody is controlled by the *Hukam*.
>
> Through the *Hukam* some achieve bliss and others are condemned to wander in transmigration.
>
> All are subject to the *Hukam*, none can escape it.
>
> Oh Nanak, if one could understand the *Hukam*, he would never be guilty of *Haumai*.
>
> (*Japjī, pauṛi* 2)

So the effect of the *hukam* is easily observable.

The path

God graciously communicates with the human heart. The voice of the *Satgurū*, the divine preceptor, is the voice heard there. The *śabad*, the word, is heard in the *man* – that place inside, the heart, where decisions are taken. The *Satgurū* communicates the *Nām*, the Name.

The effort which a person has to make and the discipline to be followed are laid down in the *bāṇī*. The pilgrimage is within. People have to understand the nature of their self-centredness, recognising that they are concerned with themselves, not God, and that because of this they remain separate, and go on wandering and suffering. 'To conquer the *man* is to conquer the world' (*Japjī*, *pauṛi* 28).

To conquer the *man*, the devotee must become *gurmukh*, and turn towards the Gurū. The Gurū mentioned in the writings of teachers like Guru Nanak is not a man but is the *Satgurū*, and this intervention is essential, because without the Gurū there is no devotion, no way in which the filth of *haumai* can be washed away.

> There is no knowledge without the Gurū.
>
> (Gurū Granth Sāhib: 469)

> Without the Gurū there can be no *bhakti* [devotion]. Without the Gurū there is no access to the company of *Sant*s. Without the Gurū one blindly engages in futile endeavour. But with the Gurū one's *man* is purified, for its filth is washed away by the word.
>
> (Gurū Granth Sāhib: 1170)

The Gurū facilitates progress, for he is the ladder, the boat, the place of pilgrimage (Gurū Granth Sāhib: 150). He gives the 'gift of the Name' (Gurū Granth Sāhib: 150). Human *gurū*s are blind; only the True Gurū can bestow the gift of the Name, and, without this, 'one comes and goes like a crow in an abandoned house' (Gurū Granth Sāhib: 58). Guru Nanak's *Asa dī Vār* is entirely concerned with the voice of the *Satgurū* in the human heart. The *Vār* consists of stanzas called *pauṛi* – literally, ladders. They are preceded by some *ślok*s. Read all, but to see the teaching of the *Vār*, omit the *ślok*s.

God is the Truth. The Gurū and the word are ways in which this can be known, and the Gurū teaches and enables humans to appropriate the Truth. If truth is to be established, the person must walk according to the *hukam* and meditate on the Name. Loving devotion must be directed towards the Lord. The love is passionate and yearning. The English word 'devotion' always sounds too weak – this love is fiery, passionate, 'soul-destroying' in getting rid of that *haumai*, painful in the intensity of yearning for the beloved. The person who is on this path suffers separation as keenly as a bereavement. The devotee must also fear God.

Nām

The *Satgurū* – the voice of God heard in the heart – is heard by *Nām simaraṇ*, remembering, meditating upon the name. Sikhism is above all the way of the Name. The Name is the Truth made manifest. It is that by which we can know God.

> Through the Name man can swim [across the Ocean of Existence]; through the Name man obtains honour and worship. The Name is man's best ornament, his intellect and his objective. Through the Name one gets recognition from others, [but] without the Name there can be no honour. All other wisdom is merely pretence; there is no fulfilment without the gift of the Name. In the Name is real power, like the power of the Government Minister, the General, and the King. Through the Name come honour and greatness which are approved [by God]. The mark of his gracious mercy [is received through the Name]. The state of immortal bliss is found in the Name, for the Name is [the proper way of] adoration. The Name is the nectar that purges the poison [of *māyā*]. Through the Name all happiness descends upon the human heart. Without the Name man is bound for the realm of death.
>
> (Gurū Granth Sāhib: 1327)

Once a person has seen that he or she has been *manmukh* and has turned toward the Gurū and the Name, then the *man*, now conquered, can become useful and take a positive role. 'He who knows himself has found the palace within' (Gurū Granth Sāhib: 56).

The five *khaṇḍs*

Many people think that the path then followed by the devotee is described by Guru Nanak as the five *khaṇḍs*, the realms or continents. However, there are many scholarly discussions and differences of interpretation of this famous passage. Some people think that the devotee passes through the *khaṇḍs* on a path similar to the *maqāmāt* of the Ṣūfīs.

The first of the *khaṇḍs* is *dharam khaṇḍ*. *Dharam* represents judgement, the law of cause and effect – God's court in fact.

God created days and nights, and the seasons of the year.
He created wind, water, fire and the regions under the earth.
In the midst of these he established earth as a place of justice.
He placed living beings of all different habits and kinds in the world.
Their names are various and endless, and they are judged according to their acts.
God and his court are true, without fault.
There those found true are accepted and honoured.
The Merciful one judges them according to their acts.
On arrival there, Oh Nanak, this shall be seen.
The bad and the good will be singled out.

(*Japjī*, *pauṛi* 34)

So earth was created as a *dharamsal* – a place for doing justice. The *khaṇḍs* are usually interpreted as a route through which the devotee passes on his journey towards the Beloved.

The second *khaṇḍ* is *giān khaṇḍ*. *Giān* means wisdom, knowledge. It is a *khaṇḍ* inhabited by many Kṛṣṇas and Śivas, many Brahmās fashioning worlds. There are many saints, moons, suns and planets. There are spiritual adepts, deities, demons and dynasties of kings. In the realm of knowledge, divine knowledge (enlightenment) shines forth.

The third *khaṇḍ* is harder to describe. *Saram khaṇḍ* presents difficulties because there are at least three different interpretations of the word *saram*. Some think that it could mean toil, effort. Others believe that it means bliss, while a third school of thought believes that it means shame, humility or surrender. An old school of thought opined that it meant practice. The context does not help. It could well be interpreted in any of the ways. *Saram khaṇḍ* is not much described, but Guru Nanak says that it is where knowledge, wisdom, intellect, and understanding, the skills of demigods and of humans of supernatural power are fashioned.

The fourth *khaṇḍ* is also hard to interpret, being the realm of *karam*. Some people think that it means grace, some think that it means *karma*, sanskritic action, and some think that it means *karam* in the sense that the devotee could earn reward. McLeod (1968: 223, 1984: 93) renders it as 'fulfilment'.

Rather than a route through which devotees rise, perhaps the words refer to the *yogas*, the paths, work, spiritual practices. *Yoga* means union with the divine. Through life on earth and judgement, through the *yogas* of *karma* (action), *giān* – *jñāna* – (knowledge), and *saram* – *dhyāna* – (effort and practice), one can strive for union. But the formless One lives in *Sach khaṇḍ*, the realm of truth. The fifth and final *khaṇḍ* is the realm of truth. 'To describe it, Nanak, is hard as steel.'

GOAL

This ultimate goal is to be sought in life – in actual experience, here and now. It is within reach, not in an after-life. The consummation of life is attainment of oneness, *jotī jot samauṇā*, mingling light with light, unity with God. If this is achieved, there is nothing more to be said. Knowing the Beloved is the only true knowledge. This is the only verification that matters and, more importantly, it is achievable and it happens during this life. This being so, we can strive towards it, experience it, and we can say something about it – although, of course, the immensity of the experience and the nature of what is experienced are ultimately beyond description. However, we can see that there have been people who have achieved this blissful state. The Gurū offered a path, a method by which it may be achieved.

Free will

'Some he calls, some he condemns to transmigrate.' There exists what McLeod (1968: 149) has described as 'doctrinal tension which is inevitable in a system upholding both the gracious activity of an absolute God and the necessary participation of man endowed with free will'.

God is all-powerful; he creates, sustains and destroys. There are statements in the *gurbāṇī* in which it appears that everything is preordained and that God does as he likes. 'He enjoys whoever He likes' (Gurū Granth Sāhib: 750). 'He alone is the bestower of union with himself' (Gurū Granth Sāhib: 20). 'No one can say anything else.' 'By the letters written on man's head his destiny is declared. He who inscribes them on others, has none on his own head. As he ordains, so shall man obtain' (*Japjī*, *pauṛi* 29).

Humans perhaps need to be reminded that ultimate decisions are not made by them; they may not presume to become united with God by their own will and effort. There is a level to which human understanding cannot aspire. On that level, God alone decides and bestows his gifts. Salvation is not acquired by mere human effort, but, 'Being self-centred we die, becoming God-centred we live' (Gurū Granth Sāhib: 1238). We can try to attune the heart towards the true, and maybe, in his kindness, God will look kindly upon us and will bestow his grace, which is often expressed as bestowing a kind glance.

> If the Kind One looks with kindness, then the true Gurū is obtained. The soul has wandered through many births, and now the true Gurū has communicated the word. There is no benefactor so great as the true Gurū: All should hear this: By meeting the true Gurū who has removed pride from the heart, and who preached the Truest of the true, the True One is obtained.
>
> (*Asa dī Vār*, *pauṛi* 4)

Perhaps it is necessary for humans to bear in mind that they do not have the ultimate power to decide the issue. It is for them to submit to the *hukam*, and doing so provides a release from *karam*. God's grace is more important than *karam* in the thought of Guru Nanak.

God's grace decides the issue. It is not acquired by mere learning, intellect, effort, or any other activity which human beings can devise. 'If a man should have thousands and hundreds of thousands of devices, Not even one would assist him in obtaining God' (*Japjī*, *pauṛi* 1).

The state to be achieved is not something known only to Sikh Gurūs; individuals in many other traditions have found illumination and have united with God, finding delight in so doing.

Conclusion

There is a story in Macauliffe (1909: vol. 2, 261) which sums up

Sikh attitudes well. There was a penitent who said, 'This is really the terrible Kal age. I a penitent bear cold and heat, yet people heed me not, while they reverence this married man as a Guru'. He 'spluttered and foamed and impotently raged'. One day he repaired to the Gurū's court and addressed him, saying, 'Sikhs are very proud; they accept not the Veds or Shastars; they make no pilgrimages; nor do they fast, perform the usual religious duties of Hindus or practise austerities of any sort. They only reverence thee and recognise thy compositions. Their adoration is confined to the utterance of Wahiguru. These misguided people are losing the advantage of their human birth. Pray tell me, sir, however can they go to heaven?' The Gurū replied:

> O Tapa, my Sikhs desire not heaven. Heaven they deem not fit reward for their merits. They never engage in worship which is merely intended for the admiration of the public. Their minds are absorbed in God's love. That is their heaven and their salvation. Thou knowest not the glory of the saints. Thou hast forsaken the real thing, attached thyself to false ceremonies, and forfeited thy salvation. Thy mind is filled with pride. Through pride and boasting men completely lose their way in this world. Without faith no devotion, penance or worship availeth. They who possess no faith are drowned in lust, wrath, worldly love, covetousness, pride, and whatever else there is of evil. It is not so with my Sikhs. Their confidence and love are reposed in the one immortal God. At every breath they repeat His name, and thus easily merit salvation. They need not penances or pilgrimages. They are in themselves pure and holy places.

FURTHER READING

Cole, W.O. and Sambhi, P.S. (1978) *The Sikhs: Their Religious Beliefs and Practices*, London, Routledge and Kegan Paul.

Doabia, Harbans Singh (1976) *Sacred nit-nem*, Amritsar, Singh Brothers.

Grewal, J.S. (1969) *Guru Nanak in History*, Chandigarh, Panjab University.

Harbans Singh (ed.) (1973) *Perspectives on Guru Nanak*, Patiala, Punjabi University.

Joshi, L.M. (ed.) (1969) *Sikhism*, Patiala, Punjabi University.

Macauliffe, M.A. (1909) *The Sikh Religion*, Oxford, Clarendon Press. Reprinted 1985, Delhi, S. Chand.

McLeod, W.H. (1968) *Guru Nanak and the Sikh Religion*, Oxford, Clarendon Press.

McLeod, W.H. (1984) *Textual Sources for the Study of Sikhism*, Manchester, Manchester University Press.
Taran Singh (1977) *Teachings of Guru Nanak Dev*, Patiala, Punjabi University.

7. Chinese Religions

Xinzhong Yao

Human nature and destiny for the Chinese is not only a religious concern but also a philosophical, an ethical and a political quest. Their searching for the answer is always in conjunction with their understanding of the relationship between the cosmos and human beings. Generally speaking, the majority of philosophical and religious schools insist that this relationship should be unitary rather than dualistic, therefore the unity of the universe (heaven) and human beings becomes a logical starting point for exploring human nature and destiny: the whole universe is a unity, and ten thousand things as well as human beings are its integral parts. Human nature is rooted in this unity and human destiny is a return to this unity.

Although there is general agreement that human beings are able to reach their ultimate goals, approaches to human nature vary in different schools of philosophy and different sects of religion. In Confucianism, the school of Mencius maintains that human nature is good and all the evils come from loss of the innately good heart, while the school of Hsun Tzu argues that human nature is innately evil and goodness is the result of cultivation and education. In Taoism, though the majority admit that human beings have partaken of the universal principle which governs the whole cosmos and therefore have the possibility of reunion with it, their proposals to purify human nature are quite different. In Buddhism, soon after its introduction from India to China, the argument about whether or not beings (especially human beings) have a *buddhata* (*buddha*-nature), and thus whether or not they are able to attain buddhahood, became a central topic among the Buddhist sects. Summarising the arguments on human nature and destiny, we find that the areas in which the Chinese have been debating concentrate on these four questions: why are human beings said to be good? what is evil? how are human beings responsible for their destiny? and what is the ideal existence for human beings?

Goodness of human nature

The main streams of Confucianism, Taoism and Buddhism hold that human nature is innately good, though their expressions of it are different. Confucianism understands the good nature as being rooted in a function of the heart, or, as Munro prefers, an 'evaluative mind' (Munro 1969: 51). Taoists insist that this goodness is a natural state which has not yet been contaminated by social culture, while the Buddhist arguments rest on the existence of *buddha*-nature in every human being, even in non-believers (*icchantikas*).

Human nature in Chinese is *jen hsing* or *hsing*. *Hsing* is composed of two parts; one is 'heart' or 'mind', which is the governing function of life, the other is 'to produce'. According to this understanding, only that which is produced from mind qualifies as human nature. Most people agree that *hsing* is unique to the species, and human nature is what makes people human beings and distinguishes them from other beings.

For most Confucians, human nature resides only in the human heart of *jen* (love, benevolence or humanity). The distinction between human beings and animals comes from human moral dignity and consciousness. With dignity and conscience, human beings become the noblest of all creatures produced by Heaven and Earth. According to Mencius, that whereby human beings differ from the birds and beasts is very small. This small thing is their good heart or mind. Mencius does not agree that the natural quality of the body is what is meant by 'nature', because even animals have desires, too. If the appetite for food and sex is human nature, how can we distinguish human beings from the birds and beasts? Human nature is a human social tendency, which is rooted in a person's innate feelings. Everybody, he argues, has an innate heart which cannot bear to see the sufferings of others. For example, if a person suddenly sees a child about to fall into a well, he or she will, without exception, experience a feeling of alarm and distress. This person feels so, not in order to win the gratitude of the child's parents, or to seek the praise of neighbours, or because of the child's cries of distress, but because it is in his or her innate nature.

This innate nature contains four senses: the sense of commiseration, the sense of shame and dislike, the sense of reverence and respect, and the sense of approving and disapproving. These four feelings are the beginnings of good – love, righteousness, propriety and wisdom. In this sense, the moral qualities are not infused into us from outside, but are in us originally (*Mencius*, Book VI, Part A, in Lau 1970: 163). Human beings have these four feelings just as they have four limbs, and they develop these four feelings into four cardinal virtues just as the nature of water is to go down and the nature of plants is to grow up. Because human beings have these beginnings of goodness within themselves, they are said to have a potential to transcend their limited life and enter the ideal realm.

Some Confucians take human nature as goodness directly from the unity between human beings and Heaven. Tung Chung-shu (179?–104? BCE) argued that human beings have a good nature because they come directly from Heaven. For him, human beings cannot create themselves, and their creator is Heaven. He described Heaven as humans' supreme father who had put the 'basic stuff' of goodness into human nature. Therefore, among all the creatures, only human beings are able to compare themselves with Heaven. This resemblance is not only present in the constitution of the human body but also in the human mind and behaviour.

> The mind possesses the power of thinking, which corresponds to [Heaven's] power of deliberation and calculation. [Humans'] conduct follows the principles of proper relationship which corresponds to the relationship between Heaven and Earth.
>
> (*Chun Chiu Fan Lu*, Chapter 13, in Fung 1952–53, vol. II: 31)

The correlation between human beings and the *jen* of Heaven has predetermined that human nature is definitely to be good.

The earlier Taoists are reluctant to use evaluative terms like 'good' and 'evil' to describe human nature, and think that these terms are created by the human mind and have no other function than corrupting human nature. The reason is obvious: if human beings concern themselves with questions of human origin, they will ignore the eternal principle within. In this respect, Taoists seem not to share the Confucian view about human nature. However, if we can gain an insight from the superficial terms into their basic attitude, we may grasp their true meaning.

In *Tao Te Ching*, *tao* and *te*, rather than *hsing*, are used to refer to the essence and characteristics of human beings. *Tao*, as the eternal principle, enters into human beings. This endowment that human beings receive from the universal principle is innate, and makes human beings hopeful. Lao Tzu names it *te*, which is usually translated as 'virtue'. However *te* is not a stationary state of virtuous habit, but an active endowment, so the ancient Chinese also interpreted it as a verb: 'to obtain'. Therefore, *te* means a special quality that one has obtained from the universal principle and then individualised in one's mentality. With this *te* in their heart, human beings are said to have obtained the true self, which is contrary to the false self humans forfeited in the social life.

Taoist masters also call for a return to one's beginning. For them, the purest and simplest – and therefore the best – stage for a human being is in childhood or, more correctly, in infancy. In *Tao Te Ching*, the newborn babe is taken as an ideal, and it is believed that by practising breathing or by embracing the ten thousand things or by following the constant *te*, one would return to being a babe (Chapters 10 and 28).

> One who possesses virtue [*te*] in abundance is comparable to a new born babe: poisonous insects will not sting it; ferocious animals will not pounce on it; predatory birds will not swoop down on it. Its bones are weak and its sinews supple yet its hold is firm. It does not know of the union of male and female yet its male member will stir: this is because its verity is at its height. It howls all day yet does not become hoarse: this is because its harmony is at its height.
>
> (*Tao Te Ching*, Chapter 55, in Lau 1963: 116)

Since the true self is, in any sense, more appreciated than the false one, and since the natural is the best, and the best is the infant, it is not odd to conclude that, for the Taoists, the innate nature of human beings is good – or at least is better than their later development.

In theory, Buddhism avoids any evaluating, because good and evil, and mind and body, are all only void and nothingness. We should, therefore, not say that Buddhists have theories about the goodness or evil of human nature. However, in fact, Chinese Buddhism is as keen as Confucianism and Taoism, if not more so, to discuss human nature, so that we can say that many Buddhist schools in China preach a theory that is not very different from those of Confucianism and Taoism. Since the third century CE, Chinese Buddhists have been arguing about whether or not there is a universal *buddha*-nature which is shared by every being. Tao-sheng (360?–434), who is regarded as a forerunner both of the Ch'an school and of the Pure Land school, insisted that all beings that had been produced by the *yin* and *yang* principles had, without exception, a *buddha*-nature. *Buddha*-nature means a possibility, reason or seed within everybody or everything. Every being, clever or foolish, righteous or villainous, follower or non-believer of Buddhism, is endowed with this seed which, if given attention, will grow and enable him or her to escape the wheel of life and death, obtain the *buddha*-wisdom (*bodhi* or *prajñā*) and enter eternity (*nirvāṇa*). This idea was later accepted by many sects of Chinese Buddhism as their first principle, and it contributed to their popularity in China.

Evil and human nature

If the universe is a natural harmony, and is imbued with a principle of goodness that provides the basis for a good nature for human beings, then where does evil come from? Why do some people develop into great persons, while others remain ordinary people and even become inferior beings?

In Chinese philosophy and religion, there seems no room for a concept of sin. Evil, both at the ontological and anthropological levels, is not given an independent position, and it is always relative to the good, as Cheng Hao (1032–1085 CE) puts it:

> The goodness and evil of the world are both equally Heavenly principles. To say that something is evil does not mean that it is inherently so. It is so merely because it either goes too far or does not go far enough.
>
> (*Erh-Cheng Yi Shu*, 2a. 2, in Fung 1952–53, vol. II: 518)

For Confucians, evil is understood as going beyond, or falling short of, the universal principle, and is some kind of deviation from the Middle Way. For Taoists, right and wrong, good and evil are all relative and interdependent concepts, and evil will arise only because the people know what is the good. For Buddhists, good and evil lie in the understanding and misunderstanding of the universe.

Consequently, for those who insist that human beings have an innately good nature, evil arises in only two ways. One is where human beings do not pay attention to their initial feelings and therefore fail to protect or cultivate the innate goodness. The other is where human beings are corrupted by their chaotic circumstances and thus the distorted heart leads to a destruction of the good nature.

Human beings have a good nature, but this nature is quite fragile and can be heavily eroded by circumstances. Mencius used a metaphor of the Ox Mountain to explain this:

> There was a time when the trees were luxuriant on the Ox Mountain. As it is on the outskirts of a great metropolis, the trees are constantly lopped by axes. Is it any wonder that they are no longer fine? With the respite they get in the day and in the moistening by the rain and dew, there is certainly no lack of new shoots coming out, but there the cattle and sheep come to graze upon the mountain. That is why it is as bald as it is. People, seeing only its baldness, tend to think that it never had any trees. But can this possibly be the nature of a mountain?
>
> (*Mencius*, Book IV, Part A, in Lau 1970: 164–5)

If human beings do not realise that they originally had a good nature, if they allow themselves to be associated with evil and do not try to look for their 'lost heart', then they will ruin their good beginning and never have the chance to become great persons.

Taoists insist that human beings have had an endowment of the universal principle and it is so-called civilisation that has corrupted the human mind. This view is revealed clearly by a story recorded in *Chuang Tzu*, in which a Taoist follower explains why he prefers simple labour to a new machine which is efficient and productive:

> Where there are machines, there are bound to be machine worries; where there are machine worries, there are bound to be machine hearts. With a machine heart in your breast, you have spoiled what was pure and simple, and without the pure and simple, the life of the spirit knows no

> rest. Where the life of the spirit knows no rest, the Way [*tao*] will cease to buoy you up.
>
> (*Chuang Tzu*, Book 12, in Watson 1968: 134)

There are others who disagree that humans are innately good, and argue that human nature is evil. Of them, Hsun Tzu is the pioneer. Hsun Tzu's understanding of human nature is completely different from that of Mencius. For Mencius, human nature is a social tendency which is inborn, but for Hsun Tzu, human nature consists of natural qualities. Though Hsun Tzu also starts with the unity between Heaven and human beings, his concept of Heaven is that of a natural cosmos. From the natural Heaven, human beings get their nature. That in human beings which is not acquired by learning and practising is what we mean by nature (*hsing*), while that in human beings which is acquired by learning and practising is called human action (*wei*). The inborn nature is nothing but human desires, emotions, feelings and instincts. These instincts, if not restrained, will certainly result in chaos. In this sense, he believes that human nature is evil, and so-called goodness – morality, propriety and righteousness – do not originally exist in human nature, but are obtained from learning, education and practices.

However, when Hsun Tzu says that human nature is evil because of desires, he seems not to mean that these desires are themselves evil. Human nature is evil because desires *will* lead to social disorder, which *is* evil. He does not, as some Taoists and Buddhists tend to, insist that, in order to change the evil nature, we must extinguish human desires and emotion. What he wants to emphasise is that it is not enough to attempt to change the evil nature by an individual's own effort. Properly satisfying one's desires needs the instructions of the sage, and therefore 'the civilising influence of teachers and laws, the guidance of the rules of proper conduct (*li*) and justice (*yi*) is absolutely necessary' (*Hsun Tzu*, Book XXIII, in Dubs 1977: 301). But, in order to accept the sage's teaching, one must have an ability to learn, to think, to practise *tao*, and this ability seems for Hsun Tzu also innate and not to be evil at all. By the outer teaching and inner learning, all people are able to change their nature, to attain their ultimate goal and to become sages.

Human responsibility for destiny

For those Confucians who insist that human nature is good, evil is not taken seriously, since evil is just the underdevelopment, deprivation, degradation or non-fulfilment of good nature. Even in ordinary people, the original goodness is not totally eradicated by their circumstances; cultivation and education should be enough to restore the good nature and to encourage its development. For those who argue that human nature is evil, the evil is also not taken seriously. Human beings, though driven by their desires, do have a basic ability to learn and to practise what the sage taught, and it is possible for people to change from the evil to the good. Thus, these two schools, with different approaches to human nature, come to the same conclusion: human beings are responsible for their own destiny, they can achieve immortality and reach the ideal life, but they also may deteriorate and descend into the abyss of evil.

Human responsibility takes two forms. In the idealistic form, individuals are expected to be responsible for their own futures. Human nature provides only a beginning, or potential. Neither the goodness nor the evil of human nature fixes human destiny, and individuals have enough room to improve their character, to change or develop their nature and to reach their ideal. Whether they actualise their potential or destroy it, and whether they reach eternity or fail to do so, it is up to each person.

The reason why inferior people become inferior is mainly that they have not realised their responsibility, have failed to develop a good heart and have not given attention to cultivating their moral sense or have let it be destroyed by evil influence. Mencius deplored the fact that people who lost their fowl and dogs knew to seek for them, but those who lost their good heart did not know to seek for it. It is urgent to awaken those people from their indulgence in bad habits and from their ignorance of their responsibility for themselves, and to lead them to the correct way to learn the *tao*.

The learning of *tao* should not be understood in the ordinary sense. As an approach to the ideal life, this learning is penetrated by a sincere attitude or integrity of the self (*cheng*). *Cheng* is the *tao* of Heaven, and to attain the *cheng* is the *tao* of human beings. Only by *cheng* can one realise one's nature, and only by realising one's nature can one be in *cheng*. A human who has absolute sincerity within is one who has attained sagehood, has been with *tao* and has reached the beyond.

> It is only he who has most *cheng* who can develop his nature to its utmost. Able to develop his own nature to its utmost, he can do the same to the natures of other men. Able to develop to their utmost the natures of other men, he can do the same to the natures of things. Able to develop things to their utmost, he can assist the transforming and nourishing operations of Heaven and Earth. Capable of assisting in those transforming and nourishing operations, he can form a trinity with Heaven and Earth.
>
> (*Chung Yung*, in Fung 1952–53, vol. I: 376)

While on the one hand the Confucian masters emphasise that one must be responsible for one's own destiny, on the other hand they do not lay all the responsibility on individuals. They have realised that there is something which is beyond one's own ability, that is, the environment – social or natural, political or religious – in which individuals grow up.

There are four kinds of so-called bad influences which are thought to have a direct effect on human nature and destiny. The first is the ignorant activities of human beings (like the hewing of trees, or browsing on the new shoots, of the Ox Mountain analogy), by which they deprive themselves or deprive each other of the good-beautiful nature. The second is the improper education and training one has received, by which a person, who should otherwise have become a sage like Yao or Yu, may become an evil person like Chieh or Chih. The third is the insufficient conditions of life under which individuals have grown up. The last, and most important, is improper government. Unlike Taoists, who search for a life retreating from the world, Confucians connect their destiny with the destiny of human beings as a whole, and thus with the fulfilment of their political ideal: curbing or objecting to or stopping evil rulers and setting up benevolent government. For them, proper or improper government would not only lead to either social harmony or chaos, but would also result in noble people or shameless people.

But, in the last analysis, the outside influences should be subject to one's own will. For firmly established persons, evil circumstances cannot change their will. Persons who have established their moral personality and devoted themselves to their ideal are called 'great humans'. 'Great humans', when obtaining the opportunity to take part in government, practise their principles for the people; and when being prevented from doing so, practise them alone; riches and honours cannot corrupt them, poverty and miserable conditions cannot change them, authority and power cannot make them bend the knee.

Taoists are even more eager to establish the concept of the responsible self in individuals. They have seen a tension between the natural and the social, between the innate and the acquired. The worldly and social life, culture and civilisation are nothing but the source of human evil. The only way for human beings to escape the corrupted world is to abandon what they have acquired from the social life, and to discard their sensory faculties. Taoists believe that whether one can or cannot achieve the ultimate goal depends upon whether or not one can cut off one's connections with the decayed world. If one appeals to one's senses and intelligence, the only thing one can expect is to run into one trouble or another and never be saved. Otherwise, if one blocks the openings (of sensing) and shuts the doors (of thinking), however one's body may decay, one will never perish. To shut the 'doors' is to retreat into one's inner world, to return to one's true self, and is a way to eternity. By this inward exploration, one may have touched the Constant: knowing the Constant, one's mind will be open; one's mind being open, one is selfless; being selfless, one is supreme; being supreme, one is divine; being divine, one is with *tao*; with *tao*, one is eternal.

Human responsibility for destiny is intensified by a dualist concept of human nature, of which one part, called the innate nature, the Heavenly nature or the benevolent nature, is good, while the other part, called the emotion, or the human desire, is evil or free to be evil or good. To develop the good nature is to curb or change one's feelings or emotions or desires, or, as Chu Hsi (1130–1200) put it, it is to clean the pearl of Heavenly nature which has become obscured by human desires.

Buddhists used the terms, 'pure nature', or the *buddha*-nature, and 'impure nature' to express the same idea.

> Not only ordinary sentient beings, but even the Buddhas, all possess the impure nature and, conversely, not only the Buddhas but even ordinary sentient beings, all possess the pure nature – the Buddha-nature.
>
> (*Mahayana Method of Cessation and Contemplation*, in Fung 1952–53, vol. II: 379)

The difference between the *buddhas* and ordinary beings is that the former have realised that the self and all other things are nothing but the products of mind, and therefore have made the pure nature of the original mind fully manifest, while the latter stick to their senses and remain in unenlightenment. To be unenlightened is to be in illusion. Breaking this illusion needs spiritual cultivation. The Buddhist cultivation includes two aspects. One is cessation, by which the practitioners will realise that the mind is the Truth. The other is contemplation, by which the cultivators will understand that all things or beings are illusionary. To reach this truth, there are two ways, the gradual way and the instantaneous way. For those Buddhists who favoured the former, in order to free the mind from its ignorance, release it from the bonds of existence, one must accumulate learning, which is the proper method to reach *buddha*-wisdom. However, according to other Buddhists who preferred the sudden way, the Buddhist teachings can only give a knowledge of the Truth, which is still outside of us. In order to attain *bodhi* (enlightenment), we have to be in the Truth and, in fact, the Truth is originally in our own mind. This is sudden enlightenment which does not need accumulation of learning and merits. According to this understanding, 'to turn one's back on delusion is to attain to the ultimate; to attain to the ultimate is to attain to the origin' (*Collected Commentaries on the Nirvâna Sutra*, vol. I, in Fung 1952–53, vol. II: 390).

The life beyond

Life is short. How can a person reach an eternal state after this life? What is this eternal state? These concerns are basically the same for Confucianism, Taoism and Buddhism.

The Confucian ideal is to achieve sagehood. The sage is not only the ideal personality but the perfection of the evolution of the whole universe. He is the bridge between humans and the universe. He can help the transformation of the cosmos, and so with Heaven and Earth he forms a trinity. In the sage, the harmony of the universe has been completely realised.

The concept of the sage gave rise to the Confucian idea of immortality. The ideal of immortality in Confucianism is neither the long-lived and never-died gods of Taoism, nor the *buddhas* who have obtained enlightenment, but a combination of inner virtue and outer achievement. This is called 'the sageness within and the kingliness without'. Why are these sage-kings regarded as the ideal life beyond? Because the sage-kings have three supreme achievements: they have illustrated virtues for ten thousand generations, by which numerous people could follow them and would not be lost in the darkness; they have created the great utilities for the nation so that the people are able to enjoy a peaceful and harmonious life; and they have created the sacred teachings which can lead human beings to their ultimate goal. By these three achievements, the sages have entered eternity, that is, though their bodily life has ceased, their spirits live forever.

Unlike the obscure terminology that Lao Tzu used to refer to the life beyond, many colourful words, vivid paragraphs and appealing books are used by other Taoists to give a clear picture of the state a person can at last reach and of the nature of the life beyond. In the *Book of Chuang Tzu* and the *Book of Lie Tzu*, we can read the detailed descriptions of the 'spiritual person', the 'perfect person' or the 'true person', which became the prototype of later Taoist immortals. The Spiritual Person does not eat the five grains, but sucks the wind, drinks the morning dew, ascends to the clouds and fogs, rides a flying dragon, and wanders over the four seas. The Perfect Person can ride the clouds and fogs, and straddle the sun and moon, and wander beyond the four seas. His eyesight is no longer limited and his vision becomes clear, and he can see all things, past–present–future. The True Person is capable of transcending the boundary of life and death, and has reached the stage of invincibility and immortality.

In religious Taoism, these descriptions were integrated into a personal concept of *hsien* – immortals. On the one hand, immortals are fully identified with the universal *tao*, on the other they have many miraculous features: they possess an indefinite prolongation of life and their bodies are invincible or imperishable, and any violence cannot harm them; they can appear young, healthy, beautiful or handsome forever, and can be transformed into any shape at their will. They also have other supernatural powers: to evoke rain, to call the wind, to create thunder and lightning.

The world for the Buddhists is an endless wheel of life and death. What they are aiming to do is to escape from this wheel and attain buddhahood. Therefore, becoming a *buddha* is the ideal life beyond.

Pure Land Buddhists, who believe that the only way to be saved is to devote themselves completely to the *buddhas*, especially Amitābha, have drawn an attractive picture of their life beyond. By the salvation of Amitābha, they will be reborn in the land of Buddha Amitābha, the *sukhāvatī* or pure land, which is situated to the west of our world. This land is rich, fertile, comfortable and beautiful. On this land there is nothing unpleasant, unwholesome, woeful or painful. Wherever they are, they can hear the *dharma* of the Buddha, the teachings of compassion, sympathetic joy, patience, tolerance and equanimity. For the followers of the Buddha, what other life could be more desirable than this?

However, life in the Pure Land seems not to be appreciated by Ch'an Buddhists. For them, *buddha*-nature is within us and the pure land is in our mind. Buddhahood is achieved by a sudden and complete enlightenment, which is a transformative experience in which one can reach a complete and thorough understanding of reality. This state is also called *nirvāṇa*. Since enlightenment is an understanding of one's own mind, so *nirvāṇa* is permanent, joyous, personal and pure. Furthermore, the enlightened person sees no difference between the self and the Truth, between humans and things; and the life in this world is at the same time the life beyond. In this sense, the enlightened or the *buddhas* are not so far from Taoist immortals and the Confucian sage. (Indeed, '*buddha*' and 'sage' were used interchangeably in many Buddhist conversations and writings.)

What we have mainly discussed above is only one aspect of the Chinese views on human nature and destiny, i.e., the humanistic aspect. There is also another aspect, i.e., the supernatural aspect. Since the earliest times, the Chinese have believed that their world is connected closely with the spiritual world, and that life and death, good and evil, wealth and poverty, whether temporary or eternal – in other words, their destiny – are primarily decided by God (*Shang Ti, T'ien*), by the ancestors and by invisible spirits. In order to reach eternal happiness, the ancient Chinese devoted themselves to God or gods, and wholeheartedly accepted whatever happened in life as their fate. However, in the last analysis, this supernatural aspect is not alien to the principle which guides the humanistic view: human nature and destiny depend upon the unity between the universe and human beings; human responsibility is to reveal this unity and correspondingly to act in accordance with this unity. On one hand, in order to understand this unity from the side of the supernatural, the Chinese developed astrology, geomancy and divination by tortoise shell or ox shoulder blades or sacred plants, to consult the will of Heaven and Earth; on the other, in order to grasp this unity from the side of human beings, they used physiognomy, chiromancy and metoposcopy to reveal the possibility and potentiality which individuals have inherited and whereby they are able to return to this unity. These beliefs and practices, though frequently condemned as superstition by Confucian orthodoxies, do constitute a supplementary understanding of the Chinese view of human nature and destiny.

FURTHER READING

Brandon, S.G.F. (1962) *Man and His Destiny in the Great Religions*, Manchester, Manchester University Press.

Chan, Wing-tsit (1963) *A Source Book in Chinese Philosophy*, Princeton, Princeton University Press.

de Bary, Wm. Theodore, et al. (ed.) (1960) *Sources of Chinese Tradition*, New York, Columbia University Press.

Dubs, H.H. (trans.) (1977) *The Works of Hsuntze*, London, Arthur Probsthain.

Fung, Yu-lan (1952–53) *A History of Chinese Philosophy*, Vols I and II, translated by Derk Bodde, London, Allen and Unwin.

Lau, D.C. (trans.) (1963) *Lao Tzu: Tao Te Ching*, London, Penguin.

Lau, D.C. (trans.) (1970) *Mencius*, London, Penguin.

Lau, D.C. (trans.) (1979) *Confucius: The Analects (Lun Yu)*, London, Penguin.

Lessa, William A. (1968) *Chinese Body Divination*, Los Angeles, United World.

Munro, Donald J. (1969) *The Concept of Man in Early China*, Stanford, Stanford University Press.

Munro Donald J. (1977) *The Concept of Man in Contemporary China*, Ann Arbor, University of Michigan Press.

Watson, Burton (trans.) (1968) *The Complete Works of Chuang Tzu*, New York, Columbia University Press.

8. Japanese Religions

Wendy Dossett

The contours of Japanese religion, despite the claim of the country to secularism, are dense and highly complex. The often noted tendency of the Japanese to eclecticism, and their propensity to re-interpret foreign belief systems until they harmonise with their own unique religious orientation, make it difficult to isolate specific themes. Generally, the different religions serve different social functions, providing rites of passage and bodies of meaning for distinct aspects of life. It presents no contradiction, for example, for most Japanese to marry in a Shinto shrine or Christian church and to want a Buddhist funeral. Also, the radical multiplication of sects and denominations since the end of World War II, and a general tendency to 'belong' to more than one, render it somewhat unrealistic to attempt to identify hermetically-sealed creeds or beliefs about human nature and destiny among the Japanese religions.

Despite this phenomenon of multi-participation, within the Japanese religions there is the struggle for self-identification. Clergy and leaders discourage practices outside the traditions of their particular religion, and engage in the task of defining their beliefs over against others. While it is difficult to see how far their apologetics are successful, they are useful for our purposes here.

Some writers have identified common themes in the wide range of Japanese religions and folk beliefs. These provide a clearer picture of Japanese religiosity and lend weight to the argument that Japanese religion can be seen as a coherent unity. Hori Ichiro (1967: 214), for example, identifies some of these as 'the emphasis on filial piety and ancestor worship . . . emphasis on *on* (debts or favours given by superiors, human or superhuman) and *hoon* (the return of *on*) . . . continuity between man and deity, or ease in deification of human beings'. In addition to these, the closeness of humanity, gods and nature is often cited as a distinctive facet of Japanese religion. This closeness manifests itself in various ways:

- the belief in *kami* (indigenous deities) with near-human passions and limitations;
- the belief in the 'apotheosis' of the dead, who, after a period of supplication and vigilance on the part of the relatives, may become *kami* or *hotoke* (*buddha*s);
- the belief in the sanctity of nature and natural forces (a belief highly compatible with the world-affirming theme within Mahāyāna Buddhism);
- the belief in the divinity or buddhahood of certain religious leaders past and present, especially, though by no means exclusively, within new religious movements;
- the belief that spiritual benefits can be reaped here and now.

Obviously there are counter-trends to the tendency of most traditions, regardless of orthodox heritage, to mediate and perpetuate these beliefs, especially among the religions which would claim absolute truth status, but the general picture remains.

The apparent blurring of the distinction between this world and the next, between human and other beings, between starting point and religious goal, is mirrored in the Japanese language itself. The duality between humans as individuals, and absolutes, is not clear-cut. The Japanese language is such that, according to Nakamura Hajime (1967: 182), there is 'heavy regard upon the relations of many individuals rather than upon the individual as an independent entity'. Arguably, the language is also resistant to the formulation of abstract concepts, absolutes and universals. Large-scale imports of logical philosophical language, notably from China, and later from Europe and America, have taken place. These have been, however, linguistic accretions, rather than anything indicative of the ability of the language and culture to express such concepts with ease. The language remains inherently non-dualistic, and, argues Nakamura (1967: 182), 'the Japanese wanted to locate the individual in experience, not in the abstract'. The nature of the language affirms the intimate relationship between humanity and the realm beyond. While the individual may hardly be a category in Japanese thought, the vast network of hierarchical relationships, both between humans, and between humans and other beings, *are* categories which are of concern to the Japanese. Here we shall examine the place of the human in some of the major traditions in Japan.

Shinto

As the indigenous and, broadly speaking, the national religion of Japan, Shinto (the Way of the Gods) has more to say about the nature and destiny of the Japanese people than about human nature in general.

Its creation myth is in respect to Japan. The Japanese Imperial family, until 1945, were sanctified by a divine lineage from the Sun Goddess, Amaterasu O Mikami, whose antecedents, Izanagi and Izanami, created Japan out of chaos. Thus the Japanese have divine justification and supremacy. The religious goal is the perpetuity of the Japanese race, crystallised in Amaterasu's command to her grandson: 'Do thou my August Grandchild, proceed thither and govern [the region]. Go! and may prosperity attend thy dynasty, and may it, like Heaven and Earth, endure forever!' (Sakamaki 1967: 26).

Connected with this belief is the emphasis on family, previously on the clan (*uji*), and on fertility. Ancestors and deceased family members, therefore, have divine status and are venerated accordingly, along with other *kami* of nature – natural forces, mountains, animals, certain trades and skills, the Japanese nation and so on.

Shinto is characterised by its celebration of life, and it dominates the rites of passage of birth and marriage. Disease, misfortune and accidental or premature death may be averted by purificatory rites and the petitioning of *kami* for health, prosperity and longevity. There is no sense of original sin; the Japanese are basically good and should prosper. Pollution (*kegare*) occurs only through neglect of ritual obligations or contact with death and disease. Generally, corpses are not permitted within shrine precincts, and traditionally, professions related to death were the preserve of the lower classes. According to Reader (1991: 68), 'The process of ritual purification and regeneration makes ideal statements about what belongs and what is desired, and what is not, separating the one from the other and creating the ideal state through which the living may most efficaciously pursue the goals of life free of spiritual hindrances'.

There is no all-embracing 'human condition' out of which the individual must rise. The individual is important only in so far as he or she is subsumed under the family group and community, will provide continuity thereof, and is a member of the Japanese race – of which the (erstwhile divine) symbol of unity is the Emperor. However, moral responsibility is clearly a requirement. One must remain unpolluted for the sake of happiness now, for the ancestors, and for future generations.

Ono Sokyo (1962: 107), using western soteriological terminology for clarification purposes, classifies 'salvation' as 'bringing the *kami* into the human world, into the daily life of the home, the market place, and the cooperation of the people'. He continues, 'Man experiences the kami in this world and salvation is attained in the harmonious development of the world'.

The realm occupied by ancestors and *kami* (*Takmaga-hara*) is not clearly delineated, although it is certainly immanent, and Reader feels (1991: 42) 'there is little real concern, beyond the wish to be at peace after death, in what lies beyond it'. Buddhism perhaps, as indicated by its funereal function, gives more substance to notions of individual destinies beyond death.

Buddhism

Along with other large-scale cultural imports from China via Korea, Buddhism was introduced into Japan in the sixth century CE. It was used primarily as a political tool. Culture from the continent was believed to be superior, and was used to validate the machinations of the ruling classes. Buddhism reaffirmed the Japanese belief in the apparently apotropaic interconnectedness of this world and the other, ritual motives being mostly the security and prosperity of the Imperial family and aristocracy, and the aversion of natural calamities. According to the Matsunagas (1976: 1), it was not until the Heian period (794–1185) that 'the transitory nature of life could be accepted as the prelude to a deeper affirmation of the nature of man'.

Until the reforms of the Kamakura period (1185–1333), Buddhism was the preserve of the aristocracy and the monasteries. Tendai and Shingon were the first to express the possibility of enlightenment for all, but Zen, Nichiren and Pure Land Buddhism –

all of which gained momentum during the Kamakura period – claimed universal enlightenment as the fulcrum of their teachings.

The Kamakura Buddhist movements were profoundly influenced by the theory of *mappo*, the Era of Degenerate Dharma. The hitherto most widely accepted teachings of the Buddha were considered no longer efficacious because of the spiritual condition of humanity in this period, bound by inexorable karmic evil. This provides a striking contrast to the positive view of human nature found within Japanese religions generally.

For Shinran (1173–1262), the founder of Jodoshinshu (the True Pure Land School), a denomination which at present claims around fourteen million adherents in Japan, the emphasis was on faith not works. One's personal effort to perform good deeds is not only worthless in this age of *mappo*, but spurious, as it implies arrogance and a clinging to the self. According to Shinran, 'priests and laymen of the Declining Age . . . being deluded by the mind of self-power to practice (*sic*) meditative and non-meditative good deeds, they are blind to the Adamantine True Faith' (Ryukoku 1983: 84). This has tremendous moral implications. Any virtue is seen as the operation of Amida Buddha through samsaric existence; there are no moral categories for humanity.

'Destiny' for Pure Land adherents is thought of as in an afterlife (*jodo*), presided over by Amida, in which the karmic conditions necessary for the attainment of enlightenment are provided. At the same time, it is possible to be reborn into the Pure Land here and now, on the basis of the identity of *saṃsāra* and *nirvāṇa*, and the ubiquity of Amida, the manifestation of absolute compassion (*daihi*). Faith in Amida's salvific powers results in this rebirth.

Jodoshinshu provides a good example of death-related practices in Japan. Its staple rituals include funeral and memorial services. Despite the founder's stress on the futility of ritual practice, it is popularly believed that the safe passage of the deceased to the Pure Land is dependent upon the vigilance of relatives, and the remembering of the deceased at services on anniversaries of the date of death. Interestingly, at such services, performed either at the temple, or in front of the *butsudan*,[1] eulogies are addressed directly to the deceased, accentuating the apparent synthesis of this world and the afterlife.

Zen, too, is primarily a funereal denomination in Japan. While its literature advocates the search for enlightenment in this life and body through the practice of meditation, insight, and the celebration of normal daily life, the average Japanese encounter with Zen (apart from through the various art forms and social rituals such as the tea ceremony) is at funerals. Although, according to Reader (1991: 84), 'not especially compatible with basic Buddhist philosophical perceptions of transience, transmigration and rebirth', Japanese folk belief in the *tama*, or soul, which continues to exist beyond this life, shapes people's beliefs about life after death even within the Buddhist context.

Zen, though, is perhaps most remarkable for its embodiment of the Mahayanist dictum '*saṃsāra* is *nirvāṇa* and *nirvāṇa* is *saṃsāra*', epitomised through its influence on the Japanese arts, which celebrate nature perfected. The 'concept' overrides logic and language, and throws the question of human nature into sharp relief. Humanity is essentially enlightened. There is no salvation from one state to another, simply realisation. For the same reason, there is no saviour, mediator, or external agent of enlightenment. Transformation takes place through the efforts of the practitioner. Enlightenment in Zen (*satori*) is attained[2] rather than bestowed.

The other dominant form of Japanese Buddhism, Nichirenism, has, at least theoretically, a more exclusivist tendency. Single-minded faith in the salvific power of the repetition of the name of the *Lotus Sūtra* is believed to bring about enlightenment in this life and body (*sokushin jobutsu* – a goal shared by Shingon Buddhism), and large-scale faith throughout the population will precipitate a utopian society. Thus, non-believers hamper this goal and are evil. According to Nichiren himself, 'Nembutsu followers will fall into the *Avici* hell, Zen followers are devils . . .' (Matsunaga 1976: 142). To Nichiren, Japan was superior among nations as it is in Japan that the enlightenment of a whole society will take place.

Nichiren placed emphasis on what can be achieved in this life, rather than looking to a spiritual realm after death. Typical of the worldly orientation of Nichirenism is the chanting for mundane benefits, seen not as somehow selfish, but as evidence of the efficacy of faith and practice. The lay movement of Nichiren Buddhism, Soka Gakkai, is involved in the United Nations and other bodies promoting peace. This highlights the utopian theme in Nichiren Buddhism, and perhaps indicates a shift in emphasis, while remaining clearly in the religious sphere, from 'spiritual' to 'political' destinies.

Confucianism

Although not an organised religion, Confucianism has played a significant role in the shaping of Japanese ideas of the nature and dignity of the human being. It lays down the ethics of human relationships: one's responsibilities to inferiors, superiors and equals, to the Imperial family and to heaven (Ch. *T'ien*, Jap. *Ten* – the Confucian concept reinforced Japanese belief in a world beyond). Among its impacts on Japanese culture, it provided the foundation of *Bushido*, the Samurai code, which continues to influence Japanese etiquette. Violation of the correct procedure in human interaction was deprecated, though there was little stress on metaphysical retribution of any kind. According to Tomikura Mitsuo (1972: 117), Confucianism was 'in the last analysis an establishment doctrine . . . people . . . were taught in effect, to stay in their place and find satisfaction in it'. However, Confucianism provides an implicit doctrine of human perfectability, and nostalgia for problem-free, harmonious existence – the Confucian religious ideal – as well as an established and integrated code of behaviour.

It is discernible in the social fabric to the present day, predominantly in the 'group ethic', and the heavy sense of contractual, social and filial obligation felt by most Japanese.

New religious movements

Deriving from Buddhism, Shinto or independent charismatics, the new religious movements in Japan span an immense spectrum of beliefs about the nature and destiny of humanity. Emphasis, however, tends to remain on the spiritual possibilities here and now; the restoration of Japan to her former or ideal harmony with *kami*, *hotoke* (deceased become *buddhas*) and ancestors; physical and mental purity; and so on. The continuity between humanity and deities is exemplified within such movements as Tenrikyo (of which the Foundress, Nakayama Miki [1798–1887], herself is believed to have been the 'shrine of god'), and Reiyukai Kyodan, which posits that human sufferings are the direct result of a discordant relationship with neglected ancestral spirits.

Tenrikyo, as well as Seicho no Ie, Sekai Kyuseikyo, and several other movements, look to a utopian society in the future through the strengthening of bonds between humanity and deities.

Christianity

Christianity has never made a significant impact on the religious life of Japan. The religion's monotheistic resistance to syncretism, and its pessimistic view of human nature in terms of original sin, are often cited as the reasons for its refusal to take root. However, its 'westernness', and its dedication to social reform, are attractive facets, and it has become a live option for about two per cent of the population – some of whom take it on strictly, while others simultaneously continue to preserve Buddhist and Shinto traditions.

In conclusion

As mentioned earlier in the chapter, from the standpoint of the ordinary Japanese, the delineations I have used between the different traditions are to some extent academic. Eclecticism is the norm, with participation across the board, and, on a philosophical level, different traditions being fused and developed to accord with whatever is seen to be in the best interests of Japanese religiosity. Universalist creeds, as in the case of Christianity, seem not to be useful, and are passively rejected. Distinctions between universal good and evil are also not recognised. Kishimoto Hideo (1967: 115) notes the 'distinct separation in the sphere of activities between the religious system and the ethical system'. 'Correct' behaviour is extolled, simply for the sake of the general well-being of the community.

Hell is not an active proposition outside the realms of superstition and crude folk belief. It is incorporated into the Buddhist world view as a provisional concept used to induce good behaviour among unenlightened beings, and into the general Japanese view as an expression of a state of mind that can be remedied here and now. Since good and evil are not objectifiable, assessment of an individual's moral or religious virtue is redundant. A notable manifestation of this is the tradition of heredity within many Japanese religions. A religious leader or member of the clergy is more often than not in his or her position simply because it runs in the family, not because of any noted dedication to the religion itself. The proper execution of the responsibilities of that position is, of course, the *summum bonum.*

Since Japanese human nature is affirmed by its glorious mythological roots, rather than denied by any notion of the taint of original sin, this world is the best of all possible worlds. Other worlds are very close and interact intimately with this one. The focus is here.

NOTES

1. A *butsudan* is a kind of 'altar' in the home. It usually contains the image of the Buddha and small memorial tablets for the family's deceased. At memorial services *sūtra*s are read in front of it. There is an equivalent altar for *kami*, often situated on the spot where the Shinto priest blessed the building of the house. Many homes have both.
2. It is, perhaps, rather inappropriate to use a word like 'attained', which implies a real distinction between two states and does not accord with basic Mahāyāna presuppositions. The emphasis, however, remains upon the efforts of the individual (*jiriki*) rather than a reliance upon 'Other Power' (*tariki*).

FURTHER READING

Hori, I. (1967) 'The Appearance of Individual Self-consciousness in Japanese Religion and Its Historical Transformations', in Charles Moore (ed.), *The Japanese Mind*, Honolulu, University of Hawaii Press.

Kishimoto, H. (1967) 'Some Japanese Cultural Traits and Religions', in Charles Moore (ed.), *The Japanese Mind*, Honolulu, University of Hawaii Press.

Matsunaga, D. and A. (1976) *The Foundation of Japanese Buddhism* (Vol. II), Tokyo and Los Angeles, Buddhist Books International.

Nakamura, H. (1967) 'Consciousness of the Individual and the Universal Among the Japanese', in Charles Moore (ed.), *The Japanese Mind*, Honolulu, University of Hawaii Press.

Ono, S. (1962) *Shintō: the Kami Way*, Rutland Vermont, Tuttle.
Reader, I. (1991) *Religion in Contemporary Japan*, London, Macmillan.
Ryukoku Translation Series (V) (1983) *The Kyō Gyō Shin Shō* – 'Teaching, Practice, Faith and Attainment' by Shinran, Kyoto, Ryukoku University.
Sakamaki, S. (1967) 'Shintō: Japanese Ethnocentrism', in Charles Moore (ed.), *The Japanese Mind*, Honolulu, University of Hawaii Press.
Tomikura, M. (1972) 'Confucianism', in *Japanese Religion* (A Survey By the Agency for Cultural Affairs), Tokyo, Kodansha.

Index